EIGHT POPES AND THE
CRISIS OF MODERNITY

RUSSELL SHAW

EIGHT POPES AND THE CRISIS OF MODERNITY

IGNATIUS PRESS   SAN FRANCISCO

The profiles of popes in this book appeared originally in a different form in the *OSV* [*Our Sunday Visitor*] *Newsweekly*.

Unless otherwise noted, the English translations of all papal documents have been taken from the Vatican website.

The translations of documents of the Second Vatican Council are from *Vatican Council II, the Conciliar and Post Conciliar Documents*, ed. Austin Flannery, O.P., rev. ed (Northport, N.Y.: Costello Publishing, 1996).

© 2020 by Ignatius Press, San Francisco
All rights reserved
ISBN 978-1-62164-340-1 (PB)
ISBN 978-1-64229-112-4 (eBook)
Library of Congress Control Number 2019947848
Printed in Canada ∞

These world crises are crises of saints.

—Saint Josemaria Escriva

CONTENTS

INTRODUCTION

Who we are as creatures, what it means to be human, why we should imagine we have any special dignity at all—these are the chronic questions behind all our anxieties and conflicts. And the answer to all of them will not be found in ideologies or the social sciences, but only in the person of Jesus Christ, redeemer of man. Which of course means we need to understand, at the deepest level, *why* we need to be redeemed in the first place.

— Archbishop Charles J. Chaput, O.F.M. Cap.[1]

Somewhere amid the chaos of the twentieth century the modern age ended. In the manner typical of this era of bloodshed and turmoil, modernity did not go quietly, but unquestionably it went. Now we live in a time of transition called "postmodern"—a nondescript word that fills a gap pending the emergence of a term to capture the special character of this new age, whatever that may turn out to be.[2]

---

[1] "Archbishop Chaput's First Synod Intervention at the Synod 2018 on Young People, the Faith, and Vocational Discernment (October 4, 2018)", ArchPhila.org, October 5, 2018 (emphasis in original). Archbishop Chaput has served successively as bishop of Rapid City, South Dakota, archbishop of Denver, and archbishop of Philadelphia.

[2] Not everyone agrees that the modern age has ended. Skeptics like the Catholic philosopher Charles Taylor believe the characteristic values and attitudes of modernity remain operative, although admittedly focused now on certain new problems and issues. I nevertheless hold with Romano Guardini and others that a new, postmodern era has indeed begun. For present purposes,

Names aside, however, the postmodern age has begun as a time of contrasts and conflicts. Pope Saint John Paul II pointed to a fundamental one of these in observing that, while some people say human beings "must now learn to live in a horizon of total absence of meaning, where everything is provisional and ephemeral", others (of a "positivist cast of mind") believe that, using tools supplied by science and technology, human beings will soon begin—indeed, already *have begun*—"completely taking charge of their destiny".[3]

In departing the stage, modernity left behind it a host of problems. Preeminent among them is one that Romano Guardini expresses thus: "Man today holds power over things, but ... he does not yet have power over his own power."[4] That is why Guardini—oddly, it may seem at first—includes earnestness on his list of "root virtues" for which there will be special need in the age to come: "For earnestness must will to know what is really at stake; it must brush aside empty rhetoric extolling progress or the conquest of nature; it must face heroically the duties forced upon man by his new situation."[5]

Of course the monumental horrors of the twentieth century had antecedents. As Guardini remarks: "A culture marked by a true ordering could not have invented such

---

however, it makes little difference which side of this argument the reader takes, since the matters with which this book is concerned will remain the same regardless of what "age" anyone situates them in.

[3] John Paul II, encyclical letter *Fides et Ratio* (September 14, 1998), no. 91.

[4] Romano Guardini, *The End of the Modern World* (Wilmington, Del.: ISI Books, 2001), 91.

[5] Ibid., 93. Monsignor Guardini, a noted Catholic theologian of the years before Vatican Council II, died in 1968, and the lectures on which his book was based were delivered in 1947–1948; but *The End of the Modern World* remains an exceptionally astute and compelling analysis of the crisis that forms the background of the events discussed in the present work.

incomprehensible systems of degradation and destruction.... What we call moral standards—responsibility, honor, sensitivity of conscience—do not vanish from humanity at large if men have not already been long debilitated."[6] In this process of debilitation, three exemplary figures stand out: Darwin, Marx, and Freud, along with the systems bearing their names. I do not suggest that these three men intended the ills of the twentieth century but only make the obvious point that their ideas contributed significantly, if unintentionally, to the decline in mankind's collective self-esteem that certainly occurred.

A word about each.

Darwin and Darwinism: Rather than being created immediately and directly by God in the image and likeness of the Creator himself, the human person was henceforth to be understood as a product of natural selection—this latter being a theory that, Charles Taylor observes, also gave "an important push towards a materialist, reductive view of the cosmos, from which all teleology was purged".[7]

Marx and Marxism: Rather than being liberated by a continuing political struggle for self-determining freedom and, on a deeper level, by the liberation from sin effected by the grace of a merciful God, human beings were henceforth to be liberated by eliminating transcendence from their lives. Jacques Maritain says of Marx that "in the scheme of [his] humanism there is no place for St. Augustine or St. Teresa of Avila, save in the measure in which they have been a moment in a dialectic whose only advance is over the dead."[8]

[6] Ibid., 86.

[7] Charles Taylor, *A Secular Age* (Cambridge, Mass.: Belknap Press of Harvard University Press, 2007), 379.

[8] Jacques Maritain, *Integral Humanism* (New York: Charles Scribner's Sons, 1968; originally published 1936), 82.

Freud and Freudianism: Rather than being intelligent agents striving to organize their lives by free choices guided by reason, human beings were now to be understood as ruled by subconscious impulses originating in perverse sexuality that impel them to act in ways over which they have no real control. Although much of the luster has worn off Freud's reputation today, the impact of Freudian theorizing lingers in popular culture and human self-understanding.

As might be expected in an intellectual climate shaped by ideas like these, atheism emerged in the last two centuries as the belief system of choice for those who considered themselves society's best and brightest. Here Friedrich Nietzsche is instructive. At the conclusion of *The Genealogy of Morals*, he writes that "unconditional honest atheism is the only air we breathe, we more spiritual men of this age ... the awe-inspiring *catastrophe* of two thousand years of training in truthfulness that finally forbids itself the *lie involved in belief in God*."[9]

If he were to return for a quick look at the present scene, Nietzsche might be dismayed to see that, by the latter years of the twentieth century, the state of mind he took in his day to be the special preserve of the "more spiritual" had filtered down in adulterated form to the common man. As Taylor puts it, "The spiritual condition of the elite became that of the masses."[10]

Other factors besides those traceable to Darwin, Marx, and Freud made their contribution to this outcome. For example, new insights in cosmology displaced earlier certainties in favor of a profound uncertainty. Where human

[9] Friedrich Nietzsche, *The Genealogy of Morals*, trans. Walter Kaufmann and R.J. Hollingdale (New York: Random House Vintage Books, 1967), 160 (emphasis in original).

[10] Taylor, *Secular Age*, 424.

beings had once seen themselves at the center of a neat, cozy cosmos in which sun and moon, planets and stars, revolved in an orderly and deferential manner around them and their planet, now they were obliged to deal with the fact that earth is an insignificant speck in a corner of an incomprehensibly vast universe—itself conceivably only one of an unknown number of universes still vaster than itself. (And meanwhile the astonishing dicta of quantum mechanics replaced what had seemed to be matter's stability with a radical condition of indetermination and randomness at the heart of physical reality.)

And then there are the recurring episodes of massive violence that were a feature of the twentieth century. During not just one but two of these, the peoples of the European nations, possessors of a high culture formed in part at least by Christian faith, flung themselves on one another with a ghastly ferocity empowered by sophisticated weaponry as if to confirm humanity's worst suspicions about itself.

Not surprisingly, bitterness and disillusionment were first fruits of the two world wars. And although David Jones' remarkable long poem *In Parenthesis* is more about the experience of combat than its consequences, bitterness is powerfully present in a passage like this:

> Give them glass eyes to see
> and synthetic spare parts to walk in the Triumphs,
>   without anyone feeling
> awkward and O, O, O, it's a lovely war with poppies
>   on the up-platform for
> a perpetual memorial of the body.[11]

---

[11] David Jones, *In Parenthesis* (New York: Chilmark Press, 1961), 176. Jones was wounded in the Battle of the Somme in July 1916 and returned to the trenches in November of that year. *In Parenthesis* was published in 1937.

As for disillusionment, it is a common theme in the literature of the period between the two world wars, with T. S. Eliot's "The Waste Land" (1922) standing as a representative, and influential, example—one that, as Taylor says, was widely seen as "an attempt to articulate our shattered condition, after the historical break".[12]

> What are the roots that clutch, what branches grow
> Out of this stony rubbish? Son of man,
> You cannot say, or guess, for you know only
> A heap of broken images.[13]

Eliot found consolation in Anglicanism. David Jones became a Roman Catholic. But many artists and intellectuals simply gave up on having faith in faith. And why not? The abandonment of faith had in fact started earlier, as Dietrich Bonhoeffer points out: "It is only when Christian faith is lost that man must himself make use of all means, even criminal ones, in order to secure by force the victory of his cause (and) the enemy, whether he be armed or defenseless, is treated as a criminal."[14]

And then there is secularism. Taylor describes its rise as a movement away from an "enchanted" world of angels and demons, magic and miracles, and a powerful sense of the sacramental, to a world of "disenchantment" closed to things of the spirit. This disenchanted world is of course the world we inhabit now. But Taylor rejects theories of "subtraction" that attempt to explain secularization as the discarding of old ideas in favor of new ones under pressure from science and rationalism. Instead, he contends, the

---

[12] Taylor, *Secular Age*, 408–9.

[13] T. S. Eliot, "The Waste Land", in *The Complete Poems and Plays of T. S. Eliot* (New York: Harcourt, Brace, 1952), 38.

[14] Dietrich Bonhoeffer, *Ethics* (New York: Macmillan, 1965), 93.

secularizing process was propelled by something altogether new that secularization itself created—a humanist mindset that looks entirely to this world for ideal human fulfillment considered as a goal reachable by unaided human effort, without reference to God or transcendence.[15]

Shades of Karl Marx! But shades also and especially of today's "transhumanism" project, which proposes to take command of evolution and, hand in hand with science and technology, create a new race of superior beings whom an articulate chronicler, Yuval Noah Harari, does not hesitate to call "gods". In the twenty-first century, Harari writes, humanity will harness genetic engineering and computer science so as to "acquire for us divine powers of creation and destruction, and upgrade *Homo sapiens* into *Homo deus*". Harari continues,

> If this sounds unscientific, or downright eccentric, it is because people often misunderstand the meaning of divinity. Divinity isn't a vague metaphysical quality. And it isn't the same as omnipotence. When speaking of upgrading humans into gods, think more in terms of Greek gods or Hindu devas rather than the omnipotent biblical sky father. Our descendants would still have their foibles, kinks and limitations, just as Zeus and Indra had theirs. But they could love, hate, create and destroy on a much grander scale than us.[16]

In other words, a next-generation version of the Nietzschean *Übermensch*.

Writers have been imagining science fiction nightmares about tinkering with human beings for a long

[15] Taylor, *Secular Age*, 15–22.
[16] Yuval Noah Harari, *Homo Deus: A Brief History of Tomorrow* (New York: HarperCollins, 2017), 47.

time: think of H. G. Wells' *The Island of Doctor Moreau*
(a mad scientist creates human-animal hybrids) or Mary
Shelley's *Frankenstein* (a scientist reanimates a corpse that
turns out to be a monster). Unlike Wells and Shelley,
however, Harari is not writing fiction. Transhumanism
might yet turn out to be the phrenology of the twenty-
first century; but Harari is describing what he considers
to be matters of fact. And the Vatican views transhumanism seriously enough that several of its offices have
tracked the issue in recent years and the Holy See hosted
a private meeting on July 29, 2019, at which specialists in
several fields discussed transhumanism under the heading
"Technology and Human Flourishing".

In fairness, however, it must be said that Harari does not
see the coming of *Homo deus* as ushering in a utopia. Rather,
in one scenario, he sees his human gods as forming a new
aristocracy engaged in dominating and exploiting an under-
class of ordinary men and women who lack the advantages
of technologically induced divinity: a new race of gods, one
might say, ruling an old race of merely human helots.

Although Bonhoeffer, writing long before transhumanism, did not see precisely all this happening, he saw
something like it in a form suited to his times—a race of
self-styled Aryan supermen, and with them the recurrence
of an ancient temptation: eat of the forbidden fruit, and
"you will be like God, knowing good and evil."[17]

> Originally man was made in the image of God, but now
> his likeness to God is a stolen one. As the image of God
> man draws his life entirely from his origin in God, but
> the man who has become like God has forgotten how he
> was at his origin and has made himself his own creator

[17] Gen 3:5.

and judge.... Instead of knowing himself solely in the reality of being chosen and loved by God, he must now know himself in the possibility of choosing and of being the origin of good and evil. He has become like God, but against God.[18]

But what does all that have to do with this book?

Eight Popes and the Crisis of Modernity is about the papacy in the twentieth century. It is not a work of history or theology or even biography, although it contains some elements of all three. It provides readers with an introduction to the eight men who occupied the highest office of the Catholic Church in troubled times and to the principal issues and problems they faced. James Chappel says correctly that the power of popes is "seldom as great as it seems" and has often been exaggerated in the writing of history;[19] yet popes really are the supreme teachers and governors in the Catholic Church, and what they say and do does tend to reflect the concerns and interests of the Church at large besides helping to create them. In short, there is no need to apologize for writing about the Catholic response to the crisis of modernity from the perspective of the papacy.

Running throughout the last century, furthermore, as well as through the story of the papacy in this time, was an overarching issue that draws a number of discrete problems together: the question of the human person. What are human beings, and how should they deal with one another? These are fundamental questions of personalism. And time and again, against the background of the events sketched above, the particular task of the Church and her

---

[18] Bonhoeffer, *Ethics*, 18–19.

[19] James Chappel, *Catholic Modern: The Challenges of Totalitarianism and the Remaking of the Church* (Cambridge, Mass.: Harvard University Press, 2018), 50.

leaders in the twentieth century was the defense, both conceptually and in fact, of human persons: their lives, their bodily integrity, their dignity, their eternal destiny. Saint John Paul II stated it explicitly in saying "man is the way for the Church."[20]

Except perhaps for John Paul, a working philosopher for much of his life and a man with a philosophical turn of mind, it would be an exaggeration to say that these eight popes spent a great deal of their time grappling directly either with what they recognized as personalist issues or with the implications of the crisis of modernity; most of the time they had their hands full dealing with other, more immediately pressing matters. But those other matters themselves were often ones generated by modernity, and questions pertaining to the dignity and destiny of the human person were at least implicit in many of them.[21]

Very briefly, and with the necessary exception of Pope John Paul I (1978), who did not live long enough to make a lasting impact on the papacy, the pontiffs and their issues were the following: Saint Pius X (1903–1914)—Modernism, a loosely linked set of ideas that he viewed (in many cases correctly) as gravely inimical to faith; Benedict XV (1914–1922)—World War I and the postwar settlement that set the stage for World War II; Pius XI (1922–1939)—the rise of totalitarianism and the assault on traditional moral

[20] John Paul II, encyclical letter *Redemptor Hominis* (March 4, 1979), no. 14.

[21] And sometimes explicit. I don't propose to compile a catalogue of twentieth-century antilife horrors here, but any such listing would obviously include the Nazi Holocaust, in which six million Jews were killed; the forced collectivization in the Soviet Union between 1929 and 1936, in which ten million died and a similar number were sent to concentration camps where many perished; Mao Tse-tung's Great Leap Forward in China during the 1950s, which cost the lives of untold millions; and the killing of millions of the unborn by abortion in the liberal democracies during the century's closing decades. And those are only a few items for what would be a very long list.

values; Pius XII (1939–1958)—World War II and the postwar threat of aggressive, antireligious Communism; Saint John XXIII (1958–1963)—bringing the Church up to date while remaining faithful to her doctrine; Saint Paul VI (1963–1978)—the implementation of Vatican Council II in the face of controversy and dissent; and Saint John Paul II (1978–2005)—the fall of the Soviet empire and the restoration of order in the Church.

Along with short profiles of these popes, the book also contains excerpts from some of their major documents, illustrating how they responded to the issues they faced, together with an overview of Vatican Council II, sketching its principal themes. *Eight Popes and the Crisis of Modernity* is a small book, but ambitious in scope.

Although none of these eight popes was infallible, except in the special sense of infallibility peculiar to popes (a pope is preserved by God from error when, speaking *ex cathedra*, he defines a doctrine of faith or morals to be held by the universal Church[22]), and each made his share of mistakes, all eight were fundamentally good men who accepted a tremendous burden in becoming pope and bore it conscientiously in the face of very difficult challenges. There is testimony to their goodness in the fact that, up to now, four of them have been formally recognized as saints. The words and deeds of all eight mirror the great issues of their times—times filled with world crises accompanying the final crisis of modernity and often threatening the life, dignity, and rights of human persons.

---

[22] Cf. DS 3074, in *Compendium of Creeds, Definitions, and Declarations on Matters of Faith and Morals*, by Heinrich Denzinger, 43rd ed., revised, enlarged, and in collaboration with Helmut Hoping, ed. Peter Hünermann for the original bilingual ed., eds. Robert Fastiggi and Anne Englund Nash for the English ed. (San Francisco: Ignatius Press, 2012), 616 (hereafter, Denzinger-Hünermann). This is the text of the definition by Vatican Council I.

At this point, however, someone may reasonably ask what I mean when I speak of the "human person". According to Chappel, this was a term of art in European Catholic circles of the 1920s, intended to "distinguish the Catholic notion of the person from the secular one".[23] That encourages me to offer the following attempt at a definition: a human person, as I use the term, is a rational animal, created by God in God's image and likeness, meant to seek flourishing in human goods for himself and others in this life, and meant by God's grace to live in the next life in eternal happiness with God. Although this very theistic account will not sit well with those who do not believe in God, looking at the matter realistically I see no way to leave him out. In the end, it seems, Pascal got it right in saying that there are three kinds of people—those who have found God and serve him, those who haven't found him but are seeking him, and those who have neither found him nor seek him: "The first are reasonable and happy, the last are foolish and unhappy; those between are unhappy and reasonable."[24]

---

[23] Chappel, *Catholic Modern*, 38.
[24] Blaise Pascal, *Pascal's Pensees*, 257 (New York: E. P. Dutton, 1958), 75.

POPE SAINT PIUS X

(August 4, 1903–August 20, 1914)

"The First Outbreak of the Modern Mind"

Coming to the throne of Peter in the early years of what was to be the bloodiest, most tumultuous century yet, Saint Pius X chose as his motto lofty, aspirational words from the epistle to the Ephesians: *Instaurare Omnia in Christo*—To Restore All Things in Christ (see Eph 1:10). Despite that motto, however, Pope Pius is best remembered today not for restoring something—although, as we shall see, he was responsible for several highly positive pastoral initiatives—but for standing firm against the inroads of a modernity devoid of faith that he saw as the deadly foe of the ancient Church. And for that, it must be said, his reputation has paid dearly.

Although he was at heart a pastor who, even as pope, taught a weekly catechism class in the shadow of the Apostolic Palace, he plainly was a pastor with a backbone of steel. That was apparent in his defiance of hostile secularism wielded as a weapon against the Church by the anticlerical government of France, and also in his determined effort to stamp out an emergent heresy that he called Modernism.

The subtitle quote is by Joseph Ratzinger, from his *Theological Highlights of Vatican II* (Mahwah, N.J.: Paulist Press, 1966), 41.

In both instances, his critics would later complain that he was too tough, too ready to fight—a view of Pius frequently repeated in liberal circles today. But the outbursts of anticlerical secularism and Modernist heterodoxy that he faced both were precursors of conflicts to come that would put successor popes to the test defending the faith against temporal powers with a fanatical hatred of the Church and self-styled reformers in the Church's own ranks agitating for a break in its life-giving continuity with its past. Half a century later, writing about the ecumenical council then underway, a young theologian who had become one of Vatican II's theological stars—Joseph Ratzinger, later Pope Benedict XVI—called Pius X's counterattack on Modernism "over-zealous"; but he also acknowledged that it was a matter of "historic necessity" in the face of a genuine threat.[1] Surely this is a better reading of the facts, not only more charitable but more just, than is the liberal opprobrium heaped on Pope Pius today.

Giuseppe Melchiorre Sarto was born on June 2, 1835, in the village of Riese in northern Italy, the second of ten children of the local postman and a seamstress. He studied in the seminary of Padua, was ordained a priest in 1858, then spent nine years engaged in pastoral work. Having served as chancellor of the Diocese of Treviso and spiritual director of its seminary, he was appointed bishop of Mantua by Pope Leo XIII in December 1884 and there proceeded to take steps to revive that moribund diocese.

In June 1893, Pope Leo named him a cardinal and patriarch of Venice. But the Italian government claimed the right to propose its own candidate for Venice and, in a move reflecting sour church-state relations dating back two decades to the Italian nationalists' seizure of the Papal

[1] Ibid., 41.

States and Rome, blocked Cardinal Sarto from assuming his new office for nine months.

Following Leo XIII's death in July 1903, his secretary of state, Mariano Cardinal Rampolla, was generally considered his likely successor. During the conclave, however, the cardinals were informed that Emperor Franz Joseph of Austria-Hungary had vetoed Rampolla. This was the last time a Catholic monarch intervened in a papal election, and historians generally concur that the imperial veto did not affect the outcome on this occasion. In any event, the voting now swung to Cardinal Sarto, who was elected pope on August 4.

The problems that faced the new pope had been accumulating for years, with France at the top of the list. Leo XIII had pursued a policy of accommodating the French government, but his approach could not move conservative French Catholics from their adamant resistance to the regime, and the Leonine policy turned out a failure in the end. Now, setting aside accommodation, Pius X and his very conservative secretary of state, Rafael Cardinal Merry del Val, were determined to fight.

So were the anticlerical rulers of France. The government had already withdrawn recognition from Catholic universities, ordered the Jesuits out of the country, required seminarians to serve in the military, and abolished chaplaincies in hospitals and the armed forces. But when Emile Combes, a bitter ex-seminarian and prominent Freemason, became prime minister, the campaign against the Church became even more intense.

In 1904 the Chamber of Deputies broke off diplomatic relations with the Holy See. The next year brought a new law on separation of church and state that ended the payment of stipends to priests in compensation for income lost at the time of the French Revolution. Church property, including churches themselves, was declared the property of the state, with its administration vested in newly established lay associations. Pius X responded by forbidding lay Catholics to cooperate in creating or operating these bodies.

Now the government moved to force bishops and priests out of their homes and seminarians out of their seminaries. Most clergy nevertheless managed to find shelter, while contributions kept a few seminaries open. And when someone asked the pope how the archbishop of Paris was supposed to get along without house, money, or church, Pius replied that when it came time to name a new archbishop, he would choose a Franciscan, since a friar, having made a vow of poverty, would already know how to live by begging.

Pope Pius and Cardinal Merry del Val are often said to have added to the tensions between the Holy See and the French government by what they said and did, and the criticism may well be correct. But historian John Pollard concludes that, even supposing Pius X had continued the accommodationist policy of Leo XIII, "it is hard to see how [the Vatican] could have avoided the rupture with France given the anti-clerical mood in that country."[2]

To some extent, nevertheless, secularism—*laïcité*, the French call it—was a blessing in disguise for the Church. For the first time in French history, indeed for the first time in any of Europe's historically Catholic countries except Ireland, the government swore off involvement in choosing bishops, leaving the pope a free hand, without interference from the state. All the same, it took World War I to bring about anything resembling reconciliation between French

[2] John Pollard, *The Papacy in the Age of Totalitarianism, 1914–1958* (Oxford: Oxford University Press, 2014), 21.

Catholicism and the anticlericals who ruled the country. In the course of that conflict, nearly 33,000 French Catholic priests served in combat as stretcher-bearers, nurses, and chaplains in the field, while another 12,500 worked in military hospitals. Of this body, 4,618 priests died in battle and over 13,000 received military decorations. In view of that record, it was impossible to question the patriotism of the French clergy.

Modernism was a challenge of a very different kind. It began among a loosely linked network of scholars and intellectuals who wished to adapt Catholicism to the currents of secular thinking of the day in Scripture studies, history, and other disciplines. Although their intentions were good, even admirable, the tendency of the Modernist spirit, as one writer remarks, was toward replacing the elements of faith with "tenets that, though culturally relevant, reflected more the philosophical fashions of the late nineteenth century than teachings of the Gospel".[3] A number of those associated with Modernism— the name was coined by Pius X, not by the Modernists themselves—undoubtedly were loyal Catholics who had no intention of doing or saying anything in conflict with the faith; but it is true nonetheless that here and there one could find ideas in circulation in Modernism that lent support to the psychologizing and relativizing of Christian faith and the debunking of its historical sources.

Modernism's two most visible and outspoken figures were a French biblical scholar, Father Alfred Loisy, and an Irish-born Jesuit, Father George Tyrrell. Calling them "tragic" individuals who "thought they could not save the

---

[3] Romanus Cessario, O.P., "Modernism", in *Our Sunday Visitor's Encyclopedia of Catholic Doctrine*, ed. Russell Shaw (Huntington, Ind.: Our Sunday Visitor Publishing Division, 1997), 450.

faith without throwing away the inner core along with the expendable shell", Joseph Ratzinger writes: "Such figures and their tragic schizophrenia show forth the mortal danger that threatened Catholicism at the first outbreak of the modern mind. They explain Pius X's uncompromising opposition to the spirit of novelty which was stirring everywhere." He quickly adds, however, that "in sifting it out, much real wheat was lost along with the chaff."[4]

Pius X's immediate response to Modernism had three parts.

On July 3, 1907, the Holy Office (predecessor of today's Congregation for the Doctrine of the Faith) issued a decree called *Lamentabili Sane Exitu* (A Lamentable Departure Indeed), condemning sixty-five propositions either taken directly from Modernist writings, or pointing to unacceptable conclusions to which Modernism was said to lead, or expressing other dubious views, said to be of a Modernist character, pertaining to biblical interpretation, Revelation, dogma, Christology, the sacraments, and the Church. Clearly objectionable propositions condemned in the decree included such statements as "the faith the Church proposes contradicts history" and "modern Catholicism can be reconciled with true science only if it is transformed into a nondogmatic Christianity; that is to say, into a broad liberal Protestantism." While it is no great stretch to see these as conclusions to be drawn from some things said by some Modernists, it was and still is debatable whether and to what extent such views were actually held by any of them at the time.[5]

Pope Pius followed *Lamentabili* on September 8, 1907, with a long encyclical called *Pascendi Domenici Gregis*

---

[4] Ratzinger, *Theological Highlights*, 41–42.

[5] See DS 3401–66. The text of *Lamentabili* can be found in Denziger-Hünermann, 689–94.

(Feeding the Lord's Flock), tracing Modernism's philosophical and theological roots to agnosticism, the philosophy of
"vital immanence", and evolutionism. The meaning
of the last two can be seen in the excerpt at the end of
this chapter; as for agnosticism, its peculiar significance in
Pius X's critique is clear in this:

> Modernists place the foundation of religious philosophy in
> that doctrine which is usually called agnosticism. Accord-
> ing to this teaching, human reason is confined entirely
> within the field of *phenomena*, that is to say, to things that
> are perceptible to the senses and in the manner in which
> they are perceptible; it has no right and no power to trans-
> gress these limits. Hence it is incapable of lifting itself up
> to God and of recognizing his existence, even by means of
> visible things. From this it is inferred that God can never
> be the direct object of science and that, as regards history,
> he must not be considered as a historical subject.
>
>   Given these premises, all will readily perceive what
> becomes of *natural theology*, of the *motives of credibility*, of
> *external revelation*. The modernists simply make away with
> them altogether.[6]

Robert Royal expresses a view of *Pascendi* that is com-
monly encountered among contemporary readers when he
says the encyclical's harsh tone and static view of Catholicism make it "difficult to like", but he also concedes that
Pius X here speaks "hard truths" and provides an accurate
"anticipation of problems" that were to emerge in Catholicism several decades later.[7]

Alfred Loisy refused to submit to the judgment expressed
in *Pascendi* and was excommunicated in 1908. He died in

[6]DS 3475–76, in Denziger-Hünermann, 695–96 (emphasis in original).

[7]Robert Royal, *A Deeper Vision: The Catholic Intellectual Tradition in the Twentieth Century* (San Francisco: Ignatius Press, 2015), 126.

1940. George Tyrrell, expelled by the Jesuits in 1906, was excommunicated in 1907 and died in 1909.

Finally, three years after the encyclical, in his motu propio *Sacrorum Antistitum* (September 1, 1910), Pius X instituted a lengthy Oath against Modernism that priests were required to take. The pope's intentions were good, but the value of such an exercise is questionable: loyal priests do not need an oath to bind them to the faith, while those perhaps not so loyal may be tempted to recite the words and then do as they please. The obligation to take the oath imposed on priests remained in force until 1967, when Pope Paul VI suspended it.

Beginning with the affirmation that the one taking the oath firmly embraces "each and every thing that is defined, proposed, and declared by the infallible teaching authority of the Church", especially "those points of doctrine that are directly opposed to the errors of this time", the text continues with propositions and affirmations like these:

> I hold with certainty and I sincerely confess that faith is not a blind inclination of religion welling up from the depth of the subconscious under the impulse of the heart and the inclination of a morally conditioned will but is the genuine assent of the intellect to a truth that is received from outside by hearing....
>
> I reject any way of judging and interpreting Holy Scripture that, disregarding the Church's tradition, the analogy of faith, and the norms laid down by the Apostolic See, adheres to the inventions of the rationalists and, with as much presumption as temerity, accepts textual criticism as the only and supreme rule.[8]

Leaving aside the question of whether requiring priests to take an oath is the best way of guaranteeing their

[8] DS 3537, 3542, 3546, in Denzinger-Hünermann, 710–11.

orthodoxy, one can at least concede that these and other declarations in the Oath against Modernism concern matters that are still required to be held and defended by the clergy and the Catholic faithful today.

Considerably more problematic, however, than these initiatives of the pope were the activities of an entity called the Sodality of Saint Pius V. Directed by a Vatican official, Monsignor Umberto Benigni, this was a clandestine network of informers whose job it was to report anyone suspected of Modernism to headquarters in Rome. Besides doing an injustice to some individuals, blighting some careers, and placing a damper on creative scholarship, this approach to eradicating Modernism not only failed to accomplish that but had the unintended consequence of driving Modernism underground, only to surface a half century later.

There was, however, more to the pontificate of Pius X than his struggles with French *laïcité* and Modernism. In several areas of Catholic life, he introduced important reforms that were to have a significant positive impact of a practical, pastoral nature. Along with steps aimed at upgrading Catholic intellectual life, restoring the Church's musical tradition, and promoting catechetical instruction, Pope Pius is remembered today for encouraging frequent, even daily, Communion and lowering the age of First Communion by children to the "age of reason".

The decree on daily reception of the Eucharist was issued by the Congregation of the Council on December 20, 1905. Attributing the hesitancy about daily Communion then existing in some quarters to a cooling of piety and the "plague of Jansenism" with its rigoristic emphasis on sin, the decree praised daily reception as a way for the faithful to "receive ... the strength to restrain passion, to wash away the little faults that occur daily, and to guard against more grievous sins".[9] As for the decree lowering the age of First Communion to "about the seventh year, more or less", it was published by the Congregation of the Sacraments and dated August 8, 1910 (*Quam Singulari*). Along with authorizing early Communion, it reminded "those who have charge over children" to "make every effort to see that these same children ... approach the holy table often and, if it can be done, daily, just as Jesus Christ and Mother Church desire".[10]

Pius X suffered a heart attack in 1913 and died of a second heart attack on August 20, 1914, shortly after the outbreak of World War I. An Anglican chronicler of the papacy writes: "In many ways deeply conservative, and so regarded by contemporaries, Pius was also one of the most constructive reforming popes. A man of transparent goodness and humility as well as resolution and organizing ability, he was spoken of as a saint and credited with miracles in his lifetime."[11] He was canonized by Pope Pius XII on May 29, 1954.

THE BATTLE AGAINST MODERNISM

Clearly it would be an exaggeration to claim Pius X as some sort of proto-personalist; yet there is a personalist element in his defense of the authenticity of faith in the anti-Modernist encyclical *Pascendi Dominici Gregis* (Feeding the Lord's Flock). For although faith does indeed involve a human need and a human reaching out to the transcendent, as Modernists maintained, it also involves, more importantly,

---

[9] DS 3375–76, in Denziger-Hünermann, 684.

[10] DS 3534, in Denziger-Hünermann, 709.

[11] J. N. D. Kelly, *The Oxford Dictionary of Popes* (Oxford: Oxford University Press, 1986), 314.

an act of divine reaching out to man that answers human
need with divine self-revelation and covenant. It is in this
reciprocity between our need and God's response that the
authenticity of the Christian's act of faith resides.

We saw Pius setting the stage for this argument in the
passage about agnosticism that was quoted above. The
thought is developed further in the excerpts from *Pascendi* that follow in which he speaks of the theory that
situates the origin of religion in human beings ("religious
immanence") and of the effects it has upon dogmas or
propositions of faith, illustrated by the example of what
science and faith respectively have to say about Christ.

> Religion, whether natural or supernatural, must, like
> every other fact, admit of some explanation. But when
> natural theology has been destroyed, the road to revelation
> closed through the rejection of the arguments of credibil-
> ity, and all external revelation absolutely denied ... it must
> be looked for in man; and since religion is a form of life,
> the explanation must certainly be found in the life of man.
> Hence the principle of *religious immanence* is formulated.
>
> Moreover, the first actuation, so to say, of every vital
> phenomenon, and religion ... belongs to this category,
> is due to a certain necessity or impulsion; but it has its
> origin ... in a movement of the heart, which movement
> is called a *sentiment*. Therefore, since God is the object of
> religion, we must conclude that faith, which is the basis
> and the foundation of all religions, consists in a sentiment
> that originates from a need of the divine.
>
> This need of the divine, which is experienced only
> in special and favorable circumstances, cannot, of itself,
> appertain to the domain of consciousness; it is at first latent
> within the consciousness, or, to borrow a term from mod-
> ern philosophy, in the *subconsciousness*. . . .
>
> We will take an illustration from the Person of Christ.
> In the Person of Christ, they say, science and history

encounter nothing that is not human. Therefore, in virtue of the first canon deduced from agnosticism, whatever there is in his history suggestive of the divine must be rejected. Then, according to the second canon, the historical Person of Christ was transfigured by faith; therefore, everything that raises it above historical conditions must be removed. Finally, the third canon, which lays down that the Person of Christ has been *disfigured* by faith, requires that everything should be excluded, deeds and words and all else that is not in keeping with his character, circumstances, and education, and with the place and time in which he lived. . . .

But the object of the *religious sentiment*, since it embraces that absolute, possesses an infinite variety of aspects of which now one, now another, may present itself. In like manner, he who believes may pass through different phases. Consequently, the formulae too, which we call dogmas, must be subject to these vicissitudes and are, therefore, liable to change. Thus the way is open to the intrinsic *evolution* of dogma. . . .

Hence should it be further asked whether Christ has wrought real miracles and made real prophecies, whether he rose truly from the dead and ascended into heaven, the answer of agnostic science will be in the negative and the answer of faith in the affirmative—yet there will not be, on that account, any conflict between them. For it will be denied by the philosopher as philosopher, speaking to philosophers and considering Christ only in his *historical reality*; and it will be affirmed by the believer, speaking to believers and considering the life of Christ as *lived again* by the faith and in the faith.[12]

---

[12] DS 3477, 3480, 3483, 3485, in Denzinger-Hünermann, 696–99 (emphasis in original).

POPE BENEDICT XV

(September 3, 1914–January 22, 1922)

"Never Was There Less Brotherly Activity"

"Are there are any Catholics here?"

Considering where this question was asked—the papal apartments overlooking St. Peter's Square—the abrupt query may have seemed rather gauche to those who heard it that day. Even so, it is a safe bet that none of them laughed. For the questioner was no less than Woodrow Wilson, the apparently all-powerful president of the United States, and the occasion was the first-ever meeting between an American president and a pope—Benedict XV.

Their encounter took place on January 4, 1919, as Wilson was making his way in triumph to Versailles for the post–World War I peace conference, an international event from which the Holy See had been excluded, despite Benedict's earnest wish that it be included as a participant. The American president's quick stopover to see the pope was probably meant as a consolation prize, offered in acknowledgment of the support that Wilson's sometimes controversial war policy had received from American

The subtitle quote is by Pope Benedict XV, in his encyclical letter *Ad Beatissimi Apostolorum* (November 1, 1914), no. 7.

Catholics under the leadership of James Cardinal Gibbons of Baltimore.[1]

Before drawing the president into his study for a private conversation, Pope Benedict said he would give his blessing to the members of Wilson's entourage. Wilson, a Presbyterian who was none too fond of the Catholic Church, looked uneasy at that. Benedict assured him the blessing would be for non-Catholics as well as Catholics, so, turning to those with him, Wilson barked out his odd question and instructed the Catholics present to step forward and get blessed. As he surely knew, that included his faithful personal secretary, the Irish American Joseph Tumulty.

As promised, Benedict blessed the group. The Catholics knelt. Wilson stayed standing, head bowed.[2]

What did these two men, so dissimilar in so many ways, Woodrow Wilson and Benedict XV, find to talk about when they were alone together after the blessing? Obviously—peace. Each had authored a set of peace proposals. Benedict's, published before the war ended, were dismissed by the Allies, who regarded them as too accommodating to Germany. Wilson intended to press his own fourteen-point plan at Versailles. As things turned out, however, the presidential plan also was set aside by the other leaders of the victorious nations in favor of a punitive settlement, designed to break Germany, that embittered the Germans and set the stage for an even deadlier war only two decades later.

[1] In fact, Gibbons had written Wilson two months before the meeting, specifically urging that, if in Rome during his European trip, he visit the pope. See John Tracy Ellis, *The Life of James Cardinal Gibbons, Archbishop of Baltimore, 1834–1921* (Milwaukee: Bruce Publishing, 1952), 2:281–82.

[2] This account of the incident is from Joseph McAuley, "Pope and President, Benedict XV and Woodrow Wilson: 'Are There Any Catholics Here?'", *America*, September 4, 2015.

Fairly or not, historians assign much of the blame for the fiasco at Versailles to Wilson and his high-minded bungling, including first of all his ill-advised decision to attend in person, thereby descending, Paul Johnson remarks, from the heights he had occupied as "most powerful man in the world" to become "just a prime minister like the rest" who lost as many arguments as he won.[3] As for Pope Benedict, the refusal of the anticlerical French and Italian governments to let the Holy See be one of the principals at Versailles had been a grievous disappointment for him. Yet, considered a century later, it looks more like a favor in disguise for the Church, since it meant that at least no one could blame the pope for the disastrous peace that was no peace that emerged from the talks.

Benedict XV is often said to be an unknown pope, but he deserves better. Heading the Church at a critical moment in world history, he responded with notable intelligence and compassion to the monumental human suffering caused by the "war to end all wars"; while his diplomacy, though not successful, nevertheless marked the Holy See's reentry into serious world affairs after a century of being shunted aside. "Though it failed to stop the war," historian John Pollard concludes, "Benedict's peace diplomacy eventually bore fruit. In the short term, it gave an immense boost to the diplomatic standing and influence of papal diplomacy, which was to be of great importance in the post-war period."[4]

Giacomo della Chiesa, the future pope, was born in Genoa on November 21, 1854, to a noble but far from

[3] Paul Johnson, *Modern Times: The World from the Twenties to the Eighties* (New York: Harper & Row, 1983), 25.

[4] John Pollard, *The Papacy in the Age of Totalitarianism, 1914–1958* (Oxford: Oxford University Press, 2014), 74.

wealthy family. The birth was premature, and the child grew up diminutive in stature and in frequent poor health. His father, a lawyer, wanted his son to follow him in the legal profession, so Giacomo obediently studied law at the University of Genoa, earning a doctorate in civil law in 1875. But then the young man's preferences prevailed and he entered the seminary, studying in Rome and receiving doctorates in theology and canon law.

Ordained a priest in 1878, he trained for the Holy See's diplomatic corps at the "Accademia"—the Academy of Noble Ecclesiastics, where young clerics preparing for careers as papal diplomats studied. While there he attracted the attention of Archbishop Mariano Rampolla, who, upon being named papal nuncio in Spain, chose the young man as his secretary.

In 1887 Pope Leo XIII named Rampolla a cardinal and appointed him secretary of state, and della Chiesa returned with him to Rome, eventually becoming undersecretary. Surprising to say, he remained in that position under Pius X and Rampolla's successor, Rafael Cardinal Merry del Val—both of them significantly more conservative than della Chiesa—until 1907, when the pope chose him to be archbishop of Bologna. The promotion was dictated, at least in part, by his superiors' desire to remove from Rome an experienced churchman whose views on policy questions were too liberal for their tastes. As it was, even though Bologna traditionally was headed by a cardinal, Vatican politics caused his elevation to be delayed until May 1914.

Pius X died just three months later, on August 20. As often is the case in papal elections, the cardinals wanted a change, and, with the war underway by then, the conclave turned to Cardinal della Chiesa as a seasoned diplomat who was known to have been at odds with the hard-line policies of the previous pope.

Inevitably, World War I and its immediate aftermath dominated the pontificate of Benedict XV, but he also found time to tend to other issues. Generally speaking, he continued the anti-Modernist line of his predecessor, though with notably less rigor. (One of his discoveries after becoming pope was that the anti-Modernist crusaders had kept a file even on him.) He promulgated the Code of Canon Law whose preparation had been initiated by Pius X. He also took steps to ease tensions with France and Italy.

In the case of France, the rapprochement included the resumption of diplomatic relations and reached its symbolic culmination in June 1920 with the canonization of the French national heroine Saint Joan of Arc. Pollard calls the healing of the rift between Paris and Rome the "crowning triumph" of the postwar diplomacy of Benedict XV and his secretary of state, Pietro Cardinal Gasparri.[5]

Things did not go as smoothly with the Italians. But under Benedict the first serious steps were taken toward resolving the "Roman question"—the estrangement of the papacy from the Italian government that dated back to 1870, when Italian nationalist troops seized Rome and Pius IX retreated behind the Vatican walls and declared himself "the Prisoner of the Vatican". Final healing of the rupture was to come in the next pontificate.

Noteworthy, too, was the apostolic letter *Maximum Illud*, issued by Benedict on November 30, 1919.[6] Here the pope set out a farsighted vision of missionary work that anticipated the end of the colonial era and signaled what Pollard calls "a revolution in the Church's missionary policy".[7] While commending foreign missionaries

---

[5] Ibid., 97.

[6] It is sometimes referred to as an encyclical, but it was not one.

[7] Pollard, *Age of Totalitarianism*, 116.

for their zeal, Benedict reminded those responsible for missions of the importance of forming native clergy. And beyond that, he wrote: "Wherever, therefore, there exists an indigenous clergy, adequate in numbers and in training ... there the missionary's work must be considered brought to a happy close." The letter also cautioned missionaries against putting their efforts at the service of the imperial ambitions of their home countries. By these standards, the pope remarked, some accounts of missionary work made "very painful reading" for they expressed "the anxiety not so much to extend the kingdom of God as to increase the power of the missionary's own country." Benedict wrote:

> Not in this way does the Catholic missionary act, who is worthy of the name; but bearing perpetually in mind that he is the ambassador, not of his own country, but of Christ, he should so comport himself that everyone can recognize in him a minister of a religion which embraces all men that adore God in spirit and truth [and] is a stranger to no nation.[8]

But above all else, it was the war that preoccupied Benedict XV and engaged the energies of the Holy See.

World War I began in 1914 amid expectations that it would not last long. "Home by Christmas," soldiers marching off to fight assured the families and friends they left behind. With a few exceptions, religious leaders in the nations directly involved in the struggle readily supported their countries' military adventures. Yet by the time the

---

[8] The English translation of *Maximum Illud* is in *Readings in Church History*, ed. Colman J. Barry, O.S.B. (Westminster, Md.: Christian Classics, 1985), 1233–42. The Vatican website provides versions in Italian, Latin, and Spanish, but not English.

conflict finally drew to a close four years later, three empires—the German, the Austro-Hungarian, and the Russian—had fallen, with a fourth, the Ottoman Empire, soon to follow. As many as ten million soldiers and sailors had died, and many more had been wounded. A prime reason for the huge loss of life was the introduction of new tools of warfare: When the war began, many military leaders took it for granted that mounted cavalry would play an important role in the fighting, while the French infantry went into battle wearing colorful bright uniforms dating back to the nineteenth century. Hardly anyone, it seems, had taken into account the murderous efficiency of the machine gun.

Historians never tire of pointing out that the Great War destroyed a European civilization that in 1914 was the envy of the world. After the fighting, Winston Churchill gave this account of it:

> Neither peoples nor rulers drew the line at any deed which they thought could help them to win. Germany, having let Hell loose, kept well in the van of terror, but she was followed step by step by the desperate and ultimately avenging nations she had assailed. Every outrage against humanity or international law was repaid by reprisals—often of a greater scale and of longer duration. No truce or parley mitigated the strife of the armies. The wounded died between the lines: the dead mouldered into the soil. Merchant ships and neutral ships and hospital ships were sunk on the seas and all on board left to their fate, or killed as they swam. Every effort was made to starve whole nations into submission without regard to age or sex.

"Torture and cannibalism," Churchill concluded, "were the only two expedients that the civilized, scientific

Christian states had been able to deny themselves, and they were of doubtful utility."[9]

Benedict XV opposed the war from the start. His first encyclical and others that followed called urgently for peace. But this is not to say the pope was indifferent to the outcome of the struggle, and in that regard the Holy See's diplomacy had three main aims: preserving the prewar status quo, and especially the survival of the Austro-Hungarian Empire as the last Catholic power among the Great Powers of Europe; propping up the Ottoman Empire as a bulwark against the expansion of Russia and Russian Orthodoxy; and keeping Italy out of the war.[10] None of these objectives was realized.

Nevertheless there was much more than this to the Holy See's wartime role under Benedict. In the face of criticism from all parties to the conflict, he refused to take sides—a policy fiercely resented by combatants who all considered themselves to be in the right. Instead, judging the war to be "a terrible manifestation of European nationalism, the collective suicide of a great Christian civilization",[11] Benedict directed a major program by the Holy See for the relief of the human suffering brought about by the fighting. These efforts included creating a special office, the Opera dei Prigioni, to collect information on prisoners of war and share it with their families, which by war's end had produced some six hundred thousand items of correspondence regarding particular prisoners; arranging for some twenty-six thousand wounded and sick men to convalesce in Switzerland; spending eighty-two million lire—a huge sum at the time that seriously strained Vatican

---

[9] Quoted in Johnson, *Modern Times*, 13–14.

[10] Michael Burleigh, *Earthly Powers* (New York: HarperCollins, Harper Perennial Edition, 2007), 457.

[11] Ibid.

finances—on humanitarian relief efforts stretching from Lithuania to Syria; and lobbying the warring governments and their leaders, including President Wilson, on behalf of peace.

Pope Benedict also displayed notable foresight in selecting two future popes for important postwar diplomatic posts—the prefect of the Vatican Library, Archbishop Achille Ratti, as legate to Poland, and Archbishop Eugenio Pacelli of the Vatican Secretariat of State as nuncio to Bavaria and, shortly, to the new German republic. Archbishop Ratti was to become Pius XI, succeeding Benedict XV. Archbishop Pacelli succeeded Pius XI as Pius XII.

And of course there was the pope's peace plan. Dated August 1, 1917, its specifics included significant arms reduction; arbitration to settle international disputes; freedom of the seas; no reparations except in special cases; restoration of the territorial integrity of Belgium and the return of other occupied territories, including German colonies; peaceful settlement of territorial conflicts; and the restoration of independence to Poland, Armenia, and the Balkan states (see excerpt below).

These steps, Benedict insisted, were needed not only to bring to an end a war that by then had become "a useless massacre" but also to prevent "the recurrence of such conflicts". Addressing national leaders at the close of his peace proposals, Pope Benedict told them: "On your decisions depend the rest and joy of countless families, the life of thousands of young people, in short, the happiness of the peoples, whose well-being it is your overriding duty to procure."[12] Although the debt was not acknowledged, some of the points in Woodrow Wilson's unsuccessful

---

[12] For the text of Benedict XV's peace proposals, see Barry, *Readings in Church History*, 1038–40.

peace plan mirrored points made by the pope. But the consensus of the victorious powers at Versailles was disastrously different from Benedict's vision: a settlement providing for harsh reparations intended to cripple Germany for years to come. The resulting treaty was formally repudiated by Adolf Hitler on March 16, 1935.

Among the scourges that followed the Great War was a devastating influenza epidemic in which many millions around the world died—far more than had died in the war itself (estimates range from twenty million to as many as one hundred million). Benedict XV contracted the disease and died on January 22, 1922, from the pneumonia that followed. Pollard writes appreciatively that during his pontificate the papacy "completely emerged from its prewar isolation" while employing its diplomatic resources not only in defense of the Church's own immediate interests but also on behalf of peace-making and humanitarian concerns. "The Holy See's ongoing, active diplomatic role in world affairs in support of peace is the most lasting legacy of his brief reign," Pollard concludes.[13]

THE ROOTS OF WAR

Dated November 1, 1914, Pope Benedict XV's first encyclical, *Ad Beatissimi Apostolorum*, appeared soon after the French halted the German advance at the Battle of the Marne and the fighting on the Western Front settled into the deadly grind of trench warfare that would drag on for four years. By the time of the encyclical's appearance, nearly a million men had died. Millions more would die before the war ended.

[13] Pollard, *Age of Totalitarianism*, 121.

Besides deploring the slaughter and pleading for its end, *Ad Beatissimi Apostolorum* offered the pope's analysis of the war's causes. Where others stressed political factors and nationalism, Benedict emphasized human factors at the roots of the vast tragedy then unfolding along with the historic folly of abandoning Christian wisdom in the direction of human affairs. The message was not unlike the one delivered by novelist Joseph Conrad only a few years earlier— the Heart of Darkness is not a place on a map but the human heart—except that Benedict, unlike Conrad, held out hope of redemption in the end. He wrote:

> But it is not the present sanguinary strife alone that distresses the nations and fills Us with anxiety and care. There is another evil raging in the very inmost heart of human society, a source of dread to all who really think, inasmuch as it has already brought, and will bring, many misfortunes upon nations, and may rightly be considered to be the root cause of the present awful war. For ever since the precepts and practices of Christian wisdom ceased to be observed in the ruling of states, it followed that, as they contained the peace and stability of institutions, the very foundations of states necessarily began to be shaken. Such, moreover, has been the change in the ideas and morals of men, that unless God comes soon to our help, the end of civilization would seem to be at hand....
>
> Our Lord Jesus Christ came down from Heaven for the very purpose of restoring amongst men the Kingdom of Peace, which the envy of the devil had destroyed, and it was His will that it should rest on no other foundation than that of brotherly love. These are His own oft-repeated words: "A new commandment I give unto you: That you love one another" (John 14:34).... And finally, as He was hanging from the cross, He poured out his blood over us all, whence being as it were compacted and fitly joined together in one body, we should love one another, with a

love like that which one member bears to another in the same body.

Far different from this is the behaviour of men today. Never perhaps was there more talking about the brotherhood of men than there is today; in fact, men do not hesitate to proclaim that striving after brotherhood is one of the greatest gifts of modern civilization, ignoring the teaching of the Gospel, and setting aside the work of Christ and of His Church. But in reality never was there less brotherly activity amongst men than at the present moment. Race hatred has reached its climax; peoples are more divided by jealousies than by frontiers; within one and the same nation, within the same city there rages the burning envy of class against class; and amongst individuals it is self-love which is the supreme law, over-ruling everything.

You see, Venerable Brethren, how necessary it is to strive in every possible way that the charity of Jesus Christ should once more rule supreme amongst men. That will ever be our own aim; that will be the keynote of Our Pontificate.[14]

Nearly three years later, on August 1, 1917, Pope Benedict published his peace plan. Its specific elements and the negative response it received have been described above. Here is its first and most notable point, in which the pope calls for the use of arbitration instead of force in settling of disputes among nations as well as for a general disarmament.

First of all, the fundamental point should be that for the material force of arms should be substituted the moral force of law; hence a just agreement by all for the simultaneous and reciprocal reduction of armaments, according to rules and guarantees to be established to the degree necessary for the maintenance of public order in each state;

---

[14] *Ad Beatissimi Apostolorum*, nos. 5–8.

then, instead of armies, the institution of arbitration, with its lofty peace-making function according to the standards to be agreed upon and with sanctions to be decided against the state which might refuse to submit international questions to arbitration or to accept its decisions.[15]

Although it is not known to have played any immediate, direct role in the pontificate of Benedict XV, one can hardly conclude this brief account of momentous events without at least some mention of what happened in 1917 at Fatima, where six times between May and October the Blessed Virgin appeared to three Portuguese peasant children, Lucia Santos and her cousins Jacinta and Francisco Marto. In the course of the apparitions, Mary delivered a message enjoining prayer and penance, especially for the conversion of Russia, and, during the apparition of July 13, presented the children with three special messages or "secrets" concerning the existence of hell, World War I and World War II, and the persecution of Christians that would happen during the century.

Although these appearances of Mary have the status of private revelations and therefore are not matters of faith, the Church recognizes their authenticity and encourages devotion to the Virgin Mary under the title Our Lady of Fatima. Jacinta and Francisco died in 1919 in the great influenza epidemic of that year and were canonized in 2017. Lucia became a Discalced Carmelite nun and died in 2005. Her cause for canonization is now underway; on February 13, 2017, she was given the title Servant of God, the first step toward canonization. Amid all the death and destruction of those momentous times a century ago, probably nothing was as important as what happened at Fatima, a remote, quiet corner of a world gone mad.

[15] Quoted in Barry, *Readings in Church History*, 1039.

POPE PIUS XI

(February 6, 1922–February 10, 1939)

Facing Up to the New Men of Violence

When Joseph Stalin, with typical brutality, sneered, "How many divisions has the pope got?" he clearly meant to underline the weakness of the papacy. Yet the question's very asking was an unintended invitation to reflect on the sources of the papacy's strength: not divisions, but prayer, diplomacy, moral truth, and the blood of martyrs.[1] Not only the papacy's worldly weakness but also its moral resources—along with, one might add, its diplomacy—were often visible during the pontificate of Pope Pius XI.

Grave crises marked his seventeen-year tenure: a world-wide economic collapse known to history as the Great Depression, the rise of totalitarian states ruled by a generation of strongmen whom one writer calls "new men of violence",[2] wars and preparations for war, and bloody persecutions of the Church even in such traditionally

---

[1] This famous question is variously said to have been put by Stalin to the French foreign minister, Pierre Laval, in May 1935 and to Winston Churchill during a conference of Allied leaders in 1944. Although the uncertainty about where and when it was asked suggests that the question may in fact never have been asked at all, it is just the sort of thing Stalin would have said if he thought of it.

[2] Michael P. Riccards, *Vicars of Christ: Popes, Power, and Politics in the Modern World* (New York: Crossroad Publishing, 1998), 129.

Catholic countries as Mexico and Spain. He died on the eve of the twentieth century's second global conflict, the most destructive in history so far, World War II.

Along with these terrible events, Pius XI was called on to face grave challenges of another kind. His years as pope coincided with unmistakable signs of an impending cultural revolution that would explode in the middle years of the century with lasting, disastrous consequences. He responded with uncompromising defenses of Catholic teaching on marriage and sexuality as well as the rights of parents and the Church in education. Trained as a scholar, Pius XI proved as pope to be a strong-willed, authoritarian leader with an explosive temper who guided the Church with a firm hand in exceedingly difficult times—a no-nonsense pontiff who once told a cardinal who said it was his duty to offer advice, "Yes, when you're asked for it."

Ambrogio Damiano Achille Ratti was born May 31, 1857, in the town of Desio, near Milan. He studied at the Gregorian University in Rome, earning doctorates in philosophy, canon law, and theology; was ordained a priest in 1879; taught at the seminary in Padua; and then began work at Milan's famous Ambrosian Library, where he served until 1911. Along with his scholarly interests, he was an avid mountain climber who scaled celebrated peaks like the Matterhorn and Mont Blanc.

In 1911 he moved to the Vatican Library, becoming its prefect in 1914. In April 1918 Pope Benedict XV surprisingly sent his head librarian on a diplomatic mission to Poland with the delicate assignment of reestablishing ecclesiastical institutions and relationships that years of German, Russian, and Austrian rule had disrupted.[3] In 1919 the

---

[3] It is possible that his linguistic skills accounted for this seemingly out-of-character assignment.

pope named him nuncio and raised him to the rank of archbishop. In 1920, during hostilities between Poland and the Soviet Union, with Warsaw apparently on the verge of falling to the Red Army, Archbishop Ratti was one of the few diplomats to remain in the city. The episode left him with a deep-seated animus against Communism.

In June 1921 Pope Benedict appointed him archbishop of Milan and made him a cardinal. Benedict died six months later, and on February 6, 1922, the cardinals chose Cardinal Ratti as pope. As his inaugural act, he delivered the traditional *Urbi et Orbi* ("to the city [Rome] and the world") blessing from the balcony of St. Peter's Basilica—the first time in half a century a pope had done that and a symbolic gesture signifying openness to improved relations with the Italian state, which had been strained since 1870 when troops of the Risorgimento, the nationalist movement for the unification of Italy, seized Rome.

As his motto, Pope Pius XI chose *Pax Christi in Regno Christi* (the Peace of Christ in the Kingdom of Christ). He spelled out its significance in the encyclical *Quas Primas* (December 11, 1925), in which he established the liturgical feast of Christ the King. "When once men recognize," he wrote, "both in private and in public life, that Christ is King, society will at last receive the great blessings of real liberty, well-ordered discipline, peace and harmony."[4] And then, the pope also clearly believed and intended that the visible Church and its head, the pope, as vicar on earth of Christ's kingly reign, would reclaim their age-old rightful role as a supranational authority guiding the course of human affairs with benevolent wisdom in the light of perennial truth.

[4] *Quas Primas*, no. 19.

The pope's preferred vehicle for realizing this ambitious vision in the secular order was the lay movement Catholic Action. His enthusiastic promotion of the group— understood according to its approved Italian model as a vehicle for the laity's participation in the hierarchy's apostolate, and thus ultimately under clerical control—earned him the title "Pope of Catholic Action". Of this papal initiative John Pollard writes: "While there were success stories for the Italian model in places like England and Wales and Australia, on the whole the most that was achieved was perhaps a keener and more general recognition of the need to organize the laity in defence of the Church."[5] But of course even this was no small thing; and it appears also to have had some success even in the United States, where existing lay organizations like the Knights of Columbus already supplied much of what Pope Pius hoped to achieve through Catholic Action, while the introduction and promotion of the latter via the bishops' National Catholic Welfare Conference and other agencies may have served to give further helpful exposure to the idea of an active lay apostolate engaged in advancing the Church's mission to the world.

Pope Pius also defended the rights of parents and the Church in education in a December 31, 1929, encyclical (*Divini Illius Magistri*) and provided a comprehensive treatment of Catholic doctrine on marriage, family, and human life in the December 31, 1930, encyclical *Casti Connubii* (excerpt below in the following section). The latter encyclical, says James Chappel, "legitimated Catholic collaboration with secular welfare states", thereby providing guidance and encouragement to Catholic activists in

---

[5] John Pollard, *The Papacy in the Age of Totalitarianism, 1914–1958* (Oxford: Oxford University Press, 2014), 237.

a number of countries who took up the promotion and protection of the family as a central theme of their efforts during the 1930s.[6]

Significantly, *Casti Connubii* appeared shortly after the Anglican bishops at the Lambeth Conference of 1930 had broken ranks with what until then had been a consensus among Christian churches in opposition to artificial birth control. Delivering the Catholic response (though without directly mentioning the Anglicans), the papal encyclical declared the wrongness of contraception in forceful terms: "Any use whatsoever of matrimony exercised in such a way that the act is deliberately frustrated in its natural power to generate life is an offense against the law of God and of nature, and those who indulge in such are branded with the guilt of a grave sin."[7]

On May 15, 1931, Pius XI made a notable contribution to Catholic social doctrine in the encyclical *Quadragesimo Anno* (the Fortieth Year—i.e., since Pope Leo XIII's groundbreaking social encyclical *Rerum Novarum* [May 15, 1891]). Published at the height of the global economic crisis—which had swiftly become a global human crisis—the papal document criticized both socialism and liberal capitalism. As an alternative it offered a corporatist vision of economic life that emphasized cooperation among classes and groups within bodies organized within particular industries and professions in preference to competition and class conflict, thus bestowing cautious praise on the experiment in corporatism then underway in Mussolini's Italy.[8] Taking their lead at least partly from

---

[6] James Chappel, *Catholic Modern: The Challenges of Totalitarianism and the Remaking of the Church* (Cambridge, Mass.: Harvard University Press, 2018), 69–78.

[7] *Casti Connubii*, no. 56.

[8] See *Quadragesimo Anno*, nos. 104–5.

the papal document, Chappel writes, "Modern forms of corporatism emerged as the dominant Catholic response to the Depression."[9]

Quadragesimo Anno also stated the principle of subsidiarity still frequently invoked by writers on politics and economics as a brake on overreaching by governments intent on social engineering and social control. "Just as it is gravely wrong to take from individuals what they can accomplish by their own initiative and industry and give it to the community," Pius XI declared, "so also it is an injustice and ... a grave evil and disturbance of right order to assign to a greater and higher association what lesser and subordinate organizations can do."[10]

Meanwhile, the pope was learning more about the practical evils of totalitarianism from events in Italy, Germany, and the Soviet Union.

Like many people, non-Italians as well as Italians, Pius XI at the start took a hopeful view of Italy's Fascist ruler, Benito Mussolini, whom he regarded as a breath of fresh air, a defender of Catholic interests and rights, and a man with whom the Church could do business—including finally resolving the by-now superannuated "Roman Question" that had roiled the Church's relations with the Italian state since the days of Pius IX. Mussolini for his part judged that a settlement with the Church would be to his advantage in a country with so many Catholics. Negotiations accordingly were quietly begun, conducted on the Church's side by Francesco Pacelli, a Church lawyer who was brother of the Vatican secretary of state, Cardinal Eugenio Pacelli. The famous Lateran Accords of 1929 were the result. In return for abandoning claims to the former Papal States

---

[9] Chappel, *Catholic Modern*, 79.
[10] *Quadragesimo Anno*, no. 79.

and Rome and recognizing the Kingdom of Italy, Vatican City was recognized as an independent state, the Holy See received the equivalent of a billion dollars in payment for its lost territories—a sum that finally set Vatican finances on a firm footing—and Catholicism was formally recognized as the religion of Italy. Pollard writes that the *Conciliazione*, as Italians called it, was "undoubtedly one of the high points of the pontificate of Pius XI and certainly his greatest achievement ... one of the key turning points in the history of the modern papacy".[11]

But despite this new relationship with the Church, the Fascists' totalitarian impulses soon asserted themselves. Soon after the signing of the accords, Mussolini himself infuriated the pope by reassuring the anticlericals in the Italian Chamber of Deputies that "the Church is not sovereign nor is it even free." To which an incensed Pius XI, speaking to the new Italian ambassador to the Holy See, responded, "Signor Mussolini has shot us in the back with a machine gun."[12] Meanwhile, the Fascists continued clamping down on Church-sponsored youth groups and on the pope's beloved Catholic Action, a process that included attacks on Catholic Action headquarters and members in various parts of the country. On June 29, 1931, Pius XI replied to these provocations with an encyclical (*Non Abbiamo Bisogno*) protesting the Fascist encroachments in angry terms and going so far as to accuse the Fascists of an outright persecution of the Church. Relations between the Holy See and the Mussolini regime remained volatile—sometimes warm, sometimes frosty—throughout the remainder of the pontificate.

---

[11] Pollard, *Age of Totalitarianism*, 158.

[12] Quoted in David I. Kertzer, *The Pope and Mussolini* (New York: Random House, 2014), 121, 125.

As these things were happening in Italy, the National Socialists in Germany were becoming an even greater source of anxiety for the Holy See. Upon coming to power in 1933, Adolf Hitler, seeing something to be gained in an agreement with the Church, pressed for a concordat in negotiations with the Vatican. No sooner was the concordat in place, however, than the Nazis began violating its terms, drawing dozens of formal protests from the Vatican in the next three years. Finally, on March 14, 1937, Pius XI published an encyclical—*Mit Brennender Sorge* (With Burning Concern)—that was smuggled into Germany and distributed secretly to priests for reading from pulpits on Palm Sunday.

Written in German, the encyclical protested not only the growing harassment of the Church but the regime's racism, including anti-Semitism, along with its aggressive neo-paganism and the myth of blood and race underlying it. As this suggests, an important though sometimes overlooked aspect of National Socialism was its character as a kind of ersatz religion, a mixture of occultism, Nordic mythology, and racist fantasizing. "The Nazi 'God'," says Michael Burleigh, "was the power of nature, conceived of as the brutal rule of the strong, with the Führer as a tangible focus for a party that was like a religious order or Church."[13] Pius XI forcefully denounced all this ominous claptrap in his encyclical, whose principal drafters were Michael Cardinal von Faulhaber of Munich and Cardinal Pacelli. Burleigh calls the result an "immensely astute critique of everything that Nazism stood for, anticipating virtually all the themes later developed by scholars of the Nazi phenomenon".[14]

---

[13] Michael Burleigh, *Sacred Causes: The Clash of Religion and Politics, from the Great War to the War on Terror* (New York: HarperCollins, 2007), 197.

[14] Ibid., 190. See the excerpt from *Mit Brennender Sorge* below.

In the Soviet Union, hostility to religion had been a prominent feature of the Communist regime from the start. "There can be nothing more abominable than religion," Lenin pronounced.[15] The Vatican for its part had sought amicable relations with the Bolsheviks in the early years of their rule, but at the same time it made the disastrous mistake of attempting to create an underground Church in the country, complete with clandestine bishops who were soon detected and eliminated.

In many people's eyes, Soviet Communism appeared to be an even greater threat to Catholicism than Nazism was, and indeed Hitler and his regime were not infrequently taken to be a bulwark against the Red menace—a role that the Führer was only too glad to play.[16] In his encyclical *Divini Redemptoris* (March 19, 1937), published within a few days of *Mit Brennender Sorge* and sounding a theme— the dignity and rights of the person—that was something of a rallying cry for Catholic social and political thought in the 1930s,[17] the pope presented a detailed critique of Communism. "Society is for man and not vice versa," and Communism erred fundamentally by reversing this right order, he declared.[18]

During the pontificate of Pius XI, bloody persecution of the Church was a grim reality in two supposedly "Catholic" countries, Mexico and Spain. Under the Mexican regime of Plutarco Elias Calles some five thousand Catholics—clergy, religious, laity—lost their lives in the

---

[15] Quoted in Paul Johnson, *Modern Times: The World from the Twenties to the Eighties* (New York: Harper & Row, 1983), 50.

[16] James Chappel points out that fear of Soviet Communism as a threat to the "West" and "Western values" was widely shared in many places in Europe by that time (see Chappel, *Catholic Modern*, 92–105).

[17] On this, see ibid., 102–3.

[18] *Divini Redemptoris*, no. 29.

1920s. As for Spain, Burleigh recalls that during the outburst of antireligious bloodletting in the early days of that country's civil war, with anarchist militias leading the way, nearly seven thousand clerics were murdered, the majority between July and December 1936, in "anticlerical atrocities that eclipsed those of the Jacobins." Over four thousand of the victims were diocesan priests, among them thirteen bishops, but they also included 2,365 male religious and 283 nuns.[19]

Pope Pius XI canonized well-known saints like Thérèse of Lisieux and Thomas More. In 1931 he founded Vatican Radio—a forward-looking move by the ancient Church to use new communication technology to carry the Gospel throughout the world.

Toward the end of the pontificate, he also grappled directly with anti-Semitism as Mussolini's government increasingly moved in that hateful direction in imitation of Nazi Germany. Pius commissioned the drafting of an encyclical on the theme (uncompleted at the time of his death), and made his views clear in a talk to Belgian pilgrims in mid-September 1938. Noting that God's promise to Abraham and his descendants was realized "through Christ", the pope declared: "Through Christ and in Christ we are Abraham's descendants. No, it is not possible for Christians to take part in anti-Semitism. Spiritually we are Jews."[20]

The pope suffered two heart attacks in November 1938 and a third, which killed him, the following February 10. During his eventful pontificate, he had faced a growing threat in the Western liberal democracies to traditional values pertaining to sexuality, marriage, and the family. He also confronted a new and distinctively modern form

---

[19] Burleigh, *Sacred Causes*, 134.
[20] Quoted in ibid., 200.

of politics combining authoritarianism and totalitarianism, with no reluctance to employ violence on a massive scale in order to achieve its objectives. Of Pius, Pollard writes laconically that "his angry outrage towards the misbehaviour of the dictators ... and his yearnings for peace all fit a personality that was essentially one of conventional Christian decency."[21] Eamon Duffy manages higher praise: "Always a strong man and an energetic pope, in the last years of his pontificate he rose to greatness. The pope of eighteen concordats ceased to be a diplomat, and achieved the stature of a prophet."[22]

THE ASSAULT ON MARRIAGE, THE MADNESS OF NAZISM

The civilizational collapse signaled by World War I was followed in the immediate postwar years by a spreading assault on traditional standards of personal morality. *Casti Connubii*, Pope Pius XI's 1930 long encyclical on marriage, contains his theological and pastoral response. The encyclical's teaching on the subject of contraception is cited above. Following are excerpts from the section in which Pope Pius sets out Catholic teaching on matrimony itself.

> Thus amongst the blessings of marriage, the child holds the first place. And indeed the Creator of the human race Himself, Who in His goodness wishes to use men as His helpers in the propagation of life, taught this when, instituting marriage in Paradise, He said to our first parents,

[21] Pollard, *Age of Totalitarianism*, 289.

[22] Eamon Duffy, *Saints and Sinners: A History of the Popes* (New Haven, Conn.: Yale University Press, 2006), 344–45.

and through them to all future spouses: "Increase and multiply, and fill the earth" (Gen 1:28)....

The blessing of offspring, however, is not completed by the mere begetting of them, but something else must be added, namely the proper education of the offspring.... Now it is certain that both by the law of nature and of God this right and duty of educating their offspring belongs in the first place to those who began the work of nature by giving them birth.... But in matrimony provision has been made in the best possible way for this education of children that is so necessary, for, since the parents are bound together by an indissoluble bond, the care and mutual help of each is always at hand....

The second blessing of matrimony ... is the blessing of conjugal honor which consists in the mutual fidelity of the spouses in fulfilling the marriage contract, so that what belongs to one of the parties by reason of this contract sanctioned by divine law, may not be denied to him or permitted to any third person; nor may there be conceded to one of the parties anything which, being contrary to the rights and laws of God and entirely opposed to matrimonial faith, can never be conceded....

This outward expression of love in the home demands not only mutual helps but must go further; must have as its primary purpose that man and wife help each other day by day in forming and perfecting themselves in the interior life, so that through their partnership in life they may advance ever more and more in virtue, and above all that they may grow in true love toward God and their neighbor....

But this accumulation of benefits is completed and, as it were, crowned by that blessing of Christian marriage which in the words of St. Augustine we have called the sacrament, by which is denoted both the indissolubility of the bond and the raising and hallowing of the contract by Christ Himself, whereby He made it an efficacious sign of grace....

Where this order of things obtains, the happiness and well being of the nation is safely guarded; what the families and individuals are, so also is the State....

When we consider the great excellence of chaste wedlock,... it appears all the more regrettable that particularly in our day we should witness this divine institution often scorned and on every side degraded.[23]

Mit Brennender Sorge, Pius XI's encyclical condemning Nazism, is dated a few years later (1937). Especially notable is the encyclical's condemnation of the peculiar blend of pagan myth, occultism, and racism lying at the rancid heart of Nazi ideology. An excerpt follows.[24]

He who replaces a personal God with a weird impersonal Fate supposedly according to ancient pre-Christian German concepts denies the wisdom and providence of God that "reacheth from end to end mightily and ordereth all things sweetly" and directs everything for the best....

This God has given his commandments in his capacity as sovereign. They apply regardless of time and space, country or race. As God's sun shines on all that bear human countenance, so does his law know no privileges or exceptions....

From the sum total of his rights as creator flows connaturally the sum total of his claims to obedience on the part of the individual and every kind of society. This claim to obedience comprehends every walk of life, in which moral questions demand a settlement in harmony with God's law and consequently the adjustment of transitory human legislation to the structures of the immutable law of God.

[23] *Casti Connubii*, nos. 11, 16, 19, 23, 31, 37, 44.

[24] The text of *Mit Brennender Sorge* from which these excerpts are taken is found in *Readings in Church History*, ed. Colman J. Barry, O.S.B. (Westminster, Md.: Christian Classics, 1985), 1211–16.

Only superficial minds can lapse into the heresy of speaking of a national God, of a national religion; only such can make the mad attempt of trying to confine within the boundaries of a single people, within the narrow blood stream of a single race, God the creator of the world, the king and lawgiver of all peoples before whose greatness all peoples are small as a drop in the bucket.

POPE PIUS XII

(March 2, 1939–October 9, 1958)

"The Modern Age in Arms"

As the first volume of Evelyn Waugh's brilliant World War II trilogy *Men at Arms* gets underway, the author introduces us to the diffident hero of this tale of bravery, betrayal, and disillusionment: Guy Crouchback, melancholy scion of an old English Catholic family, and to Crouchback's jaundiced view of recent history (which, very likely, was much the same as Waugh's). Like nearly everyone else, Waugh writes, Guy has seen war coming for years and has taken it for granted that when there was no more avoiding the need to fight, feckless England would stumble into battle "in a panic, for the wrong reasons or for no reason at all".[1]

Then comes August 23, 1939, with its stunning news: Nazi Germany and the Soviet Union, bitter foes till then, have entered into a nonaggression pact, thus setting the stage for their twin invasions of Poland and the commencement of war. Crouchback greets this development with grim joy, as a man who has at last found his raison d'etre: "Now, splendidly, everything had become clear.

The subtitle quote is by Evelyn Waugh, in his *Men at Arms* (Boston: Little, Brown, 1952), 8.

[1] Ibid., 7.

The enemy at last was plain in view, huge and hateful, all disguise cast off. It was the Modern Age in arms. Whatever the outcome there was a place for him in that battle."[2]

Historians record the significance of this act of profound mutual cynicism by the Nazis and the Soviets more prosaically: "The Molotov-Ribbentrop Non-Aggression Pact of August 1939 prepared the way for World War II and Stalin's first serious attempt at imperial expansion. He calculated that a treaty with Germany would provoke a major European war, a war that he wanted to last as long as possible. Soviet archives have revealed that Stalin planned to dominate Europe with the help of Hitler's war machine and then eliminate Germany 'as a rival for total hegemony over the continent.'"[3] This of course is perfectly accurate. But Waugh's version—the modern age in arms—cuts to the truth of the matter at a different, deeper level.

And this was the world crisis that the cardinals gathered in conclave six months before had been anticipating when they chose Eugenio Pacelli—Pope Pius XII—to head the Church Militant as 259th successor of Saint Peter.

In many ways, he was superbly prepared for the task by his years in the diplomatic service of the Holy See and as Vatican secretary of state. Eamon Duffy writes: "He was elected, as everyone knew, to be Pope in a time of total war, a role for which everything about his career— his diplomatic skills, his gift of languages, his sensitivity and intelligence—all equipped him."[4] From another perspective, however, it is doubtful whether Eugenio Pacelli or anyone else could have been adequately prepared for

---

[2] Ibid., 7–8.

[3] Lee Edwards and Elizabeth Edwards Spalding, *A Brief History of the Cold War* (Washington, D.C.: Regnery Publishing, 2016), 11.

[4] Eamon Duffy, *Saints and Sinners: A History of the Popes* (New Haven, Conn.: Yale University Press, 2006), 345–46.

the stupendous challenges and burdens of office that this ascetic, refined, highly sophisticated man soon would face as leader of a worldwide Church that herself was being put to the test in a world at war. All things considered, he rose to the occasion remarkably well.

Eugenio Maria Giuseppe Giovanni Pacelli was born March 2, 1876, one of four children of a family of the "Black Nobility"—the name popularly given to those old Roman families who, loyal to the papacy in good times and bad, frequently held posts in the service of the Holy See. His grandfather had been an official of the Papal States under Pius IX and a founder of the Vatican newspaper, *L'Osservatore Romano*; his father, dean of the Roman Rota; his brother, Francesco, a legal advisor to Pius XI and principal negotiator on the Church's side of the Lateran Accords, which established the terms of the relationship between the Holy See and the Italian state after decades of estrangement.

Eugenio was ordained a priest in 1899. After a brief period of pastoral work, he joined the staff of the Vatican Secretariat of State and worked with Pietro Cardinal Gasparri on the preparation of the first-ever Code of Canon Law, which went into effect in 1918. During these years, he frequently represented the Holy See at international events including in 1911 the coronation of Britain's King George V. When Pope Benedict XV in 1914 chose Cardinal Gasparri as his secretary of state, the cardinal chose Father Pacelli to head the secretariat's section on "extraordinary ecclesiastical affairs"—in effect, the Holy See's foreign office. During World War I, the priest directed the Vatican's massive and highly successful programs for locating and assisting prisoners of war and distributing humanitarian aid.

In 1917 Pope Benedict appointed him nuncio to Bavaria and made him an archbishop. In Munich during

the ascendancy of the short-lived Bavarian Soviet republic, he faced down a band of armed Marxist revolution-
aries, an experience that, Duffy says, "marked him for life
with a deep fear of socialism in all its forms".[5] In 1920 the
pope named him nuncio to the new German republic,
and in 1925 he moved to Berlin. Also during these years,
Archbishop Pacelli represented the Holy See in secret talks
with representatives of the Soviet Union with the hope of
finding a modus vivendi for the Church in that officially
atheistic country. In the absence of progress, however,
Pius XI ordered the talks terminated in 1927. Shortly after
the global financial crisis of 1929 that signaled the onset
of the Great Depression, the pope recalled him to Rome,
made him a cardinal, and, when Cardinal Gasparri retired,
appointed him secretary of state.

In that capacity Cardinal Pacelli traveled widely. Seeing
him as a likely successor, Pope Pius told one of the cardinal's assistants in the Secretariat of State that he "made
him travel 'so that he may get to know the world and
the world may get to know him'".[6] One of those jour-
neys, in 1936, took him to the United States, where the
trip's logistics were organized by Auxiliary Bishop Francis Spellman of Boston (later, archbishop of New York
and a cardinal), a friend from the days when the two men
had served together in the Secretariat of State. With fund-
ing provided by Boston multimillionaire (and father of a
future president) Joseph P. Kennedy, Cardinal Pacelli and
Bishop Spellman flew across the United States in a char-
tered airliner.[7] Among his stops during this unusual trip,
the cardinal met with President Franklin D. Roosevelt

[5] Ibid., 346.
[6] Ibid., 345.
[7] Russell Shaw, *Catholics in America* (San Francisco: Ignatius Press, 2016), 90.

at the Roosevelt family home in Hyde Park, New York. Roosevelt thereafter referred to him as "my old friend", and in 1939 the president named former U.S. Steel executive Myron Taylor to be his personal representative to the Holy See. The White House and the Vatican were to communicate often during the war years.[8]

As secretary of state, Cardinal Pacelli was a believer in concordats—formal treaties setting out the terms of relationships between the Church and the secular state—and negotiated these with numerous countries, notably including Germany, where Adolf Hitler saw political advantage in an agreement with the Church. The cardinal for his part had no illusions about the Nazis but hoped to obtain for the Church the protection afforded by a mutually agreed treaty. But Nazi violations of the concordat began almost at once, and during the next four years Cardinal Pacelli signed over seventy formal protests to the German government. In 1937, together with Michael Cardinal von Faulhaber of Munich, he had a large hand in writing *Mit Brennender Sorge*, Pius XI's encyclical condemning National Socialism's pagan ideology. This, the first official condemnation of Nazism by any major group, drew a vengeful response from the Nazis, including a series of trials of Catholic priests accused of immorality.[9]

As Pius XI had expected, after the old pope's death in February 1939, the cardinals took Cardinal Pacelli to be his logical successor. Elected on March 2, he chose as his motto *Opus Justitiae Pax* (Peace, the Work of Justice). True to those words, one of his first official acts was to call

[8] See Michael P. Riccards, *Vicars of Christ: Popes, Power, and Politics in the Modern World* (New York: Crossroad Publishing, 1998), 135–38.

[9] Michael Burleigh, *Sacred Causes: The Clash of Religion and Politics, from the Great War to the War on Terror* (New York: HarperCollins, 2007), 190.

for an international conference to head off war. His first encyclical, *Summi Pontificatus*, issued in the same year on October 20, after the fighting had begun, condemned the German and Soviet invasions of Poland, anti-Semitism, and totalitarianism.

In the face of war, Pope Pius followed the Vatican's traditional policy of official neutrality. It is now known, however, that in 1940 he served as a channel between German military leaders contemplating a coup to overthrow Hitler and the British government, and that he passed on to the Allies information that he had received indicating that the German attack on the Low Countries was imminent.

As it had done during the First World War, during this conflict, too, the Vatican carried on a large-scale program of humanitarian relief, especially to prisoners of war. Pope Pius gave asylum in the Vatican and at Castel Gandolfo to many persons seeking refuge, among them many Jews. Numerous convents in Rome did the same. Repeatedly he pleaded for Rome to be treated as an "open city" and spared Allied bombing, and when bombs fell just the same on the city's largest cemetery, demolishing the tombs of the Pacelli family, he rushed to the scene to comfort the injured and bless the dead and dying.

Although Pope Pius XII despised Nazism and regarded Hitler as an evil man, he held Soviet Communism to be an even greater menace to the Church and Western civilization. Following the war, therefore, he was deeply concerned about the spread of Communism in Eastern Europe, imposed and supported by the Red Army, while fearing its continued expansion westward. In 1948 and again in 1950, seeking to block Communist victory in Italian elections—an outcome that seemed entirely possible at the time and that, had it occurred, would have been a huge setback for both the Church and democracy—he called on Catholics to turn out and vote, while threatening Communists and those who supported them with excommunication. The Communists lost, not solely but certainly in part due to the pope's efforts.

During these years, the Church behind the Iron Curtain suffered grievously at Communist hands. Pollard sums up the "terrible assault" in these words: "The Church came under attack in the Baltic States, Poland, Czechoslovakia, Hungary, Romania, Bulgaria, Albania, and Yugoslavia. Very similar policies were applied in all these countries, based on the ideology of atheistic materialism and the Soviet experience of three decades of the 'Godless campaigns'".[10] This was the era of the Church of Silence, of show trials and imprisonment of Church leaders like Cardinal Wyszynski (Poland), Cardinal Stepinac (Yugoslavia), Cardinal Beran (Czechoslovakia), and Cardinal Mindszenty (Hungary), and of continuing Communist efforts to control and harass believers. Writers who now shrug off this persecution and belittle Pope Pius' resolute anti-Communism apparently have short memories.

Although now best remembered for his role in the world crises of his day, Pius XII also made notable contributions to Catholic doctrine and liturgy. These included the encyclical on the Mystical Body of Christ *Mystici Corporis Christi* (June 29, 1943), the encyclical on promoting biblical studies *Divino Afflante Spiritu* (September 30, 1943), and the encyclical on the sacred liturgy *Mediator Dei* (November 20, 1947), as well as the reform of the Holy Week liturgy and the shortening of the eucharistic fast. In such ways he laid the groundwork for the Second Vatican Council two decades later. Very different, however, was

[10] John Pollard, *The Papacy in the Age of Totalitarianism, 1914–1958* (Oxford: Oxford University Press, 2014), 366.

the encyclical *Humani Generis* (August 12, 1950), which criticized some philosophical and theological trends of the day as reflected in the writings of several theologians who a few years later were to have a major influence on Vatican Council II. In 1950 Pope Pius infallibly defined the dogma of the Blessed Virgin's bodily Assumption into heaven. In talks to numerous groups, he applied Catholic moral principles to contemporary issues and developments ranging from motion pictures to biomedical ethics.

Like his predecessor, Pius XII conducted his pontificate in a notably centralized manner, with teaching and administrative authority flowing downward from the papacy to lower levels of the hierarchy; the idea of collegiality—the ecclesiastical equivalent of limited power-sharing between pope and bishops—would have to wait for the Second Vatican Council. Pollard, no great admirer of this pope, nevertheless calls it the "ultimate irony" that many forces that at Vatican II were to converge in putting an end to major features of Catholicism as it was in the first half of the twentieth century "were actually generated in that period itself and, in large part by, the very pope, Pius XII, who most especially symbolized that kind of Catholicism".[11]

Starting with a long illness in 1954, Pope Pius' health declined, and he became increasingly isolated, withdrawn, and authoritarian. He died on October 9, 1958. Pope Benedict XVI declared him "Venerable" in 2009.

No account of Pius XII would be complete without a few words about the pope and the Jews.

---

[11] Pollard, *Age of Totalitarianism*, 478. This is an assessment that can be taken, among other things, as confirming that, along with some obvious discontinuity, the Catholicism of the century's second half was in fundamental continuity with the Catholicism of the first—an important point, as we shall see, in forming a proper assessment of Vatican Council II itself.

To begin with, the image of Pius as "Hitler's pope" is fantasy. There is no serious doubt about the mutual dislike between Pope Pius and the Nazis. On a number of occasions, as relations worsened, Hitler said he would "deal with" the pope, and there was even talk of having him kidnapped, although nothing came of it.[12] The excerpts below, from Pius' first encyclical, *Summi Pontificatus*, reflect a vision of human solidarity that was to be fundamental to his view of the Holocaust and much else. And in the postwar years he was looked upon as a "moral icon" throughout Europe.[13]

Yet for some years now he has been criticized for supposedly not sufficiently denouncing the Nazi persecution of Jews. The origin of this charge can be found in a 1963 play, *The Deputy*, by a left-wing German writer named Rolf Hochhuth, in which the pope is depicted as a greedy hypocrite. But Pius XII also has many defenders, and British historian Michael Burleigh calls him a target of "Communist-inspired denigration".[14]

There are nevertheless legitimate questions here. Did Pius XII say enough about the agony of the Jews? But what would "enough" have been in the circumstances of those times? His most substantial wartime comment on this matter came in his radio message to the world for Christmas 1942. This five-thousand-word text, carefully prepared by the pope, calls on listeners who are "magnanimous and upright" to join in vowing to build a just and decent social order when peace is restored. Humanity "owes that vow", he said, to several groups: those who have died in

---

[12] Pollard, *Age of Totalitarianism*, 395.

[13] James Chappel, *Catholic Modern: The Challenges of Totalitarianism and the Remaking of the Church* (Cambridge, Mass.: Harvard University Press, 2018), 147.

[14] Burleigh, *Sacred Causes*, 293, 361.

battle; the mothers, widows, and orphans of the dead, exiles, and refugees; noncombatants killed, injured, and rendered homeless by indiscriminate bombing; and to a group whom he describes in these words: "The hundreds of thousands of persons who, without any fault on their part, sometimes only because of their nationality or race, have been consigned to death or a slow decline."[15]

As Pope Pius saw it, that was a clear and forceful condemnation of the Nazi assault of the Jews. Others contend that it was not specific enough or strong enough; but the Nazis knew who was being criticized and for what, and they were furious about it, as Eamon Duffy points out: "Both Mussolini and the German Ambassador, von Ribbentrop, were angered by this speech, and Germany considered that the Pope had abandoned any pretence at neutrality. They felt that Pius had unequivocally condemned Nazi action against the Jews."[16] Moreover, the example of the bishops of Holland offered Pope Pius good grounds for fearing that repeated public denunciations would do more harm than good. Encouraged by the papal Christmas message, the Dutch bishops publicly condemned the Nazi assault on the Jews of the Netherlands; and the effect of this forceful condemnation was to provoke still more violent and vicious Nazi action against the suffering Dutch Jews.

It seems unlikely that this argument will end anytime soon. Duffy remarks that the literature on the subject is "bewildering in its bulk, its virulence, and its lack of

[15] "1942 Christmas Address of Pope Pius XII", in "Text of Pope Pius XII's Christmas Message Broadcast from Vatican to the World", *New York Times*, December 25, 1942, https://www.nytimes.com/1942/12/25/archives/text-of-pope-pius-xiis-christmas-message-broadcast-from-vatican-to.html. The Vatican's website carries the text of the 1942 Christmas address but only in Italian, Portuguese, and Spanish.

[16] Duffy, *Saints and Sinners*, 348.

consensus",[17] and Pollard says: "Such is the nature of the dispute over Pius XII's response to the Holocaust that one seriously doubts whether it is a genuine historiographical controversy"—rather, in this experienced historian's estimate, it appears to be "a highly *political* dispute" between Catholics and Jews in the United States, as well as between liberal and conservative Catholics.[18] It is reasonable to think that a different pope in the same position as Pius XII—a Pius XI, say, or a John Paul II—might have responded very differently, with very different results for the Jews and the papacy alike. But along with being different, would those results have been any better or might they instead have been even worse? Who really knows? Pope Pius XII did what he believed was right; he was responsible for saving many Jews,[19] and Jewish leaders after the war praised and thanked him for it—while the chief rabbi of Rome, Israel Zolli, upon converting to Catholicism in February 1945, chose as his baptismal name Eugenio.

THE UNITY OF HUMAN SOCIETY

Pope Pius XII's first encyclical *Summi Pontificatus* is dated October 20, 1939—not quite seven months after his election as pope and less than two months after the German invasion of Poland. It carries the subtitle "On the Unity of Human Society".

---

[17] Ibid., 451.

[18] Pollard, *Age of Totalitarianism*, 5–6 (emphasis in original).

[19] How many? In the nature of things, it is not possible to give an exact figure. "At the time," Duffy notes, "he was credited within having saved tens of thousands of Jewish lives" (Duffy, *Saints and Sinners*, 347–48), and it is probably best to leave it at that.

Along with lamenting the outbreak of war, which he had done his best to prevent—by trying without success to organize a peace conference involving Britain, France, Germany, Italy, Poland, and perhaps even the United States, as well as by issuing repeated appeals to the potential belligerents to settle their differences peacefully[20]— Pope Pius offered an analysis of the conflict's causes that also was an implicit prescription for preventing more such clashes in the future.

The overriding cause, he argued, lay in the breakdown of human solidarity, and specifically in racism and statism; in the context of the times, Pollard writes, these papal strictures "could only apply to Nazi Germany and, to a lesser extent, Fascist Italy".[21] A lasting solution, Pius XII reasoned, could only be found in the restoration of solidarity grounded in the Christian vision of humanity's fundamental unity. He wrote:

> Among the many errors which derive from the poisoned source of religious and moral agnosticism, We would draw your attention, Venerable Brethren, to two in particular, as being those which more than others render almost impossible or at least precarious and uncertain, the peaceful intercourse of peoples.
>
> The first of these pernicious errors, widespread today, is the forgetfulness of that law of human solidarity and charity which is dictated and imposed by our common origin and by the equality of rational nature in all men, to whatever people they belong, and by the redeeming Sacrifice offered by Jesus Christ on the Altar of the Cross to His Heavenly Father on behalf of sinful mankind....
>
> In the light of this unity of all mankind, which exists in law and in fact, individuals do not feel themselves isolated

---

[20] See Pollard, *Age of Totalitarianism*, 300–303.
[21] Ibid., 309.

units, like grains of sand, but united by the very force of their nature and by their internal destiny, into an organic, harmonious mutual relationship which varies with the changing of times.

And the nations, despite a difference of development due to diverse conditions of life and of culture, are not destined to break the unity of the human race, but rather to enrich and embellish it by the sharing of their own peculiar gifts and by that reciprocal interchange of goods which can be possible and efficacious only when a mutual love and a lively sense of charity unite all the sons of the same Father and all those redeemed by the same Divine Blood. . . .

But there is yet another error no less pernicious to the well-being of the nations and to the prosperity of that great human society which gathers together and embraces within its confines all races. It is the error contained in those ideas which do not hesitate to divorce civil authority from every kind of dependence upon the Supreme Being—First Source and absolute Master of man and society—and from every restraint of a Higher Law derived from God as from its First Source. . . .

To consider the State as something ultimate to which everything else should be subordinated and directed, cannot fail to harm the true and lasting prosperity of nations. This can happen either when unrestricted dominion comes to be conferred on the State as having a mandate from the nation, people, or even a social order, or when the State arrogates such dominion to itself as absolute master, despotically, without any mandate whatsoever.[22]

[22] *Summi Pontificatus*, nos. 34–35, 42–43, 52, 60.

POPE SAINT JOHN XXIII

(October 28, 1958–June 3, 1963)

The Provisional Pope Who Launched a Revolution

It's said that when Angelo Cardinal Roncalli boarded the train in Venice on his way to Rome for the conclave of cardinals that would choose the successor to Pius XII, he had his return ticket in his pocket. It's also said that when he entered the conclave, he knew he had a good chance of leaving it as pope. If both things are true—and there is no reason to suppose they aren't—the ticket in the pocket expressed Cardinal Roncalli's humility, while the awareness that he might well be elected pope reflected the hard-headed realism of someone who had seen a great deal of the world. And also, needless to say, of the Church.

That fusion of humility and realism can be seen in retreat notes written three years later by the man who by then was known to the world as Pope John XXIII:

When on 28 October, 1958, the cardinals of the Holy Roman Church chose me to assume the supreme responsibility of ruling the universal flock of Jesus Christ at 77 years of age, everyone was convinced that I would be a provisional and transitional pope. Yet here I am ... with an immense program of work in front of me to be carried out before the eyes of the whole world, which is watching and waiting. As for me, I feel like St. Martin [of Tours], who "neither feared to die, nor refused to live."[1]

The centerpiece of that "immense program" was of course the Second Vatican Council.

For the preceding four hundred years, Catholic life had largely adhered to the pattern laid out by the sixteenth-century Council of Trent, a great reforming council that put in place sweeping policies and programs embodying the Catholic response to the Protestant Reformation. The pattern provided by Trent proved to be remarkably effective and durable. But times change, and by the middle years of the twentieth century the feeling was growing in progressive Catholic circles that the Church also needed to change. Then came Pope John and his council, launching a new era in the Church, with consequences that are still unfolding.

The man with whom it all began was born November 25, 1881, in Sotto il Monte, a village near Bergamo in northern Italy, third of thirteen children in a family of farmers. He was a bright youth who entered the seminary and, after studies in Bergamo, received a scholarship to study in Rome, where he was ordained in 1901. His subsequent career included serving as secretary to the bishop of Bergamo, hospital orderly and army chaplain during World War I, and national director of the Propagation of the Faith organization in Italy.

In 1925 Pope Pius XI named him an archbishop and appointed him apostolic visitor to Bulgaria, a post in which he remained until 1934. During his years in Sofia he was often lonely and suffered from feeling he was not accomplishing

---

[1]John XXIII, "Retreat in the Vatican from 27 November–3 December, 1960", in *Journal of a Soul* (New York: New American Library, 1966), 353.

much. "My prolonged mission as papal representative in this country often causes me acute and intimate suffering," he confessed in retreat notes for 1933.[2] In November 1934, however, he was appointed apostolic delegate to Turkey and Greece, and once war broke out he had his hands full with humanitarian concerns that included helping thousands of Jews who were fleeing the Nazis. Paul Johnson writes in his biography that Archbishop Roncalli's contacts with the German ambassador, Franz von Papen, "ensured that the German embassy made little effort to interfere in the mercy-traffic in Jews".[3] As war raged, the apostolic delegate in Istanbul drew his own conclusions, and in retreat notes from 1940 he included patriotism among those things from which he prayed especially to be delivered; patriotism is "right and may be holy", he wrote, but it "may also degenerate into nationalism". He continues,

> The world is poisoned with morbid nationalism, built up on the basis of race and blood, in contradiction to the Gospel. In this matter especially, which is of burning topical interest, "deliver me from men of blood, O God". Here fits in most aptly the invocation: "God of my salvation"; Jesus our Saviour died for all nations, without distinction of race or blood, and became the first brother of the new human family, built on him and his Gospel.[4]

After Istanbul came Paris—the prestigious, sensitive post of nuncio to France, where he served from 1944 to 1953. Among other things, he succeeded in persuading the French government to reduce from twenty-three to two the number of bishops it wanted removed for having

---

[2] Ibid., 279.
[3] Paul Johnson, *Pope John XXIII* (Boston: Little, Brown, 1974), 58–59.
[4] John XXIII, *Journal of a Soul*, 309.

been overly friendly during the war to the collaborationist Vichy regime.[5] He also helped bring about the settlement of disputes over schools and the manner of appointing bishops and left France amid expressions of good will on all sides.

In June 1953 Pius XII named him cardinal and patriarch of Venice. Arriving there, he asked the Venetians to be "indulgent to a man who wants simply to be your brother, loving, approachable, understanding".[6] Assuming that this would be his last posting, he enjoyed his years in Venice and the opportunity they gave him to concentrate on being a pastor. That pastoral reputation preceded him into the conclave of October 1958, and there the cardinals, looking for a change from the lofty, patrician style of Pius XII, and also looking for an interim pope whose advanced years made it unlikely he would remain in office much longer than it took them to sort out their thinking about the future direction of the Church, entrusted the See of Peter to the personable, eminently pastoral seventy-seven-year-old patriarch of Venice. He took the name John and chose as his motto *Obedientia et Pax* (Obedience and Peace).

And the cardinals certainly got their change. So did the rest of the Church.

To begin with, there were his looks and his manner. "Whereas Pius XII was tall, thin, aloof, austere, and aristocratic," James Hitchcock writes, "John was short, rotund, and informal, given to making jokes at his own expense." More than that, he "deliberately departed from papal protocol by the kinds of guests he received", among them the

---

[5] On Archbishop Roncalli's career as nuncio, see Johnson, *Pope John XXIII*, 59–75.

[6] Quoted in ibid., 79.

Anglican archbishop of Canterbury and Soviet Premier Nikita Khrushchev's atheist son-in-law.[7] A natural ecumenist, he established a Vatican office for Christian unity and reached out in friendship to Jews.

Along with the quips and the kindliness, however, there was also that immense program, unveiled to a small group of startled cardinals three months after his election. Its items: a synod for the Diocese of Rome (a pope is, after all, bishop of Rome), an updated Code of Canon Law for the Western Church, and, most immense undertaking of all, an ecumenical council.

The Roman synod was held a year later and is generally thought not to have accomplished anything very remarkable. The Code of Canon Law, a genuinely significant achievement, was completed in 1983 and promulgated by Pope Saint John Paul II. As for the ecumenical council, it opened in October 1962 and closed in December 1965, after four momentous sessions. Vatican II is widely regarded as the most important Catholic event—indeed, perhaps the most important *religious* event—of the twentieth century.

Pope John later said the idea of convoking a council had come to him suddenly, as if by inspiration. There is no reason to believe otherwise; but the possibility of reconvening Vatican Council I, which was not formally closed when deliberations were broken abruptly off in 1870, had in fact been seriously considered as far back as the pontificate of Pope Pius XI, was revived in the years of Pius XII, and was discussed by Cardinal Roncalli with other cardinals on the eve of his election as pope.

Catholics still disagree about whether Vatican II was needed. Earlier councils generally were summoned to deal

---

[7] James Hitchcock, *History of the Catholic Church* (San Francisco: Ignatius Press, 2012), 474.

with particular problems calling for urgent solutions. The Council of Trent, which instituted reforms in response to the Protestant Reformation, is a notable instance. By contrast, in the middle years of the twentieth century, Catholicism appeared to most people to be stable and strong, and Catholics, so far as anyone could tell, were satisfied with their Church as it was. So what problem or problems was an ecumenical council supposed to solve?

Although it's sometimes said Pope John failed to provide an answer to that question, his answer in fact is clearly stated in his speech to the twenty-four hundred bishops assembled in St. Peter's at the council's opening session on October 11, 1962. The problem may not be that he provided no answer, but that the answer he provided is so radically simple, involving as it does the essential mission of the Church.

Much has been written about that remarkable opening address, with special attention given to John's criticism of "prophets of doom"—presumably, certain cardinals of the Roman Curia who were said to look with jaundiced eyes upon a world they viewed as growing steadily worse— as well as to John's call for aggiornamento, updating, in the manner of presenting the Church's doctrine, though certainly not in the doctrine itself. But something still more basic came first. "The great problem confronting the world after almost two thousand years remains unchanged," John declared, and this was the great problem that Pope John looked to the ecumenical council to solve.

Certain it is that the critical issues, the thorny problems that wait upon men's solution, have remained the same for almost twenty centuries. And why? Because the whole of history and of life hinges on the person of Jesus Christ. *Either* men anchor themselves on Him and His Church, and thus enjoy the blessings of light and joy, right order and peace; *or* they live their lives apart from Him; many positively oppose Him, and deliberately exclude themselves from the Church. The result can only be confusion in their lives, bitterness in their relations with one another, and the savage threat of war.[8]

Here, then, was John XXIII's challenge to the ecumenical council: aggiornamento, yes, but in tandem with *ressourcement*—a return to the spiritual and doctrinal sources of Christianity—so as to preach Jesus Christ and his message convincingly to a world that so desperately needed them. How well Vatican II succeeded in meeting this challenge to upgrade and expand its efforts to bring the good news of Christ to the modern world will be debated for years to come.

Two encyclicals also stand as milestones of John's pontificate: *Mater et Magistra* (Mother and Teacher), dated May 15, 1961, and *Pacem in Terris* (Peace on Earth), which carries the date April 11, 1963, less than two months before his death.

Mater et Magistra irked some Catholic economic and social conservatives who took to saying, "Mater, sì. Magistra, no" (Mother, yes. Teacher, no). But the document nevertheless stands as Pope John's principal contribution to Catholic social doctrine. After quick summaries of the social philosophy of Leo XIII, Pius XI, and Pius XII, the encyclical calls for workers' participation in ownership of the companies they work for—a familiar trope of earlier Catholic social documents—while declaring an

[8]John XXIII, "Opening Address to the Council", CatholicCulture.org, 2019, https://www.catholicculture.org/culture/library/view.cfm?RecNum=3233. (The Vatican website vatican.va provides versions in Italian, Latin, Portuguese, and Spanish, but not English.)

economic system that exploits workers to be "altogether unjust—no matter how much wealth it produces, or how justly and equitably such wealth is distributed".[9] *Mater et Magistra* also speaks of the universal destination of goods, a principle that has been a central part of Catholic social teaching since that time, while linking it to private ownership of property:

> But it is not enough to assert that the right to own private property and the means of production is inherent in human nature. We must also insist on the extension of this right in practice to all classes of citizens....
>
> Our predecessors have insisted time and again on the social function inherent in the right of private ownership, for it cannot be denied that in the plan of the Creator all of this world's goods are primarily intended for the worthy support of the entire human race.[10]

Pacem in Terris had its origin at least partly in what may have been the most terrifying episode of the entire Cold War. In October 1962, as the ecumenical council was getting underway, the world held its breath while the Cuban Missile Crisis propelled the United States and the Soviet Union to the brink of nuclear war. John XXIII is credited with playing a crucial role in mediating that confrontation, and the events of those days likely contributed to shaping the peace encyclical.

Along with calling for negotiations leading to a ban on nuclear weapons,[11] *Pacem in Terris* is notable for its lengthy enumeration of individual human rights and the obligations to which they give rise, a passage reminiscent of the

---

[9] *Mater et Magistra*, no. 83.
[10] *Mater et Magistra*, nos. 113, 119.
[11] *Pacem in Terris*, no. 112.

Universal Declaration on Human Rights adopted by the
United Nations General Assembly in 1948, and perhaps
partly meant to revive some of the optimistic idealism
that accompanied that earlier document. The encyclical's
personalism is strikingly present in its formulation of the
"one fundamental principle" that it says should underlie
all human relationships: every human individual is "truly a
person". The pope continues,

> His is a nature, that is, endowed with intelligence and
> free will. As such he has rights and duties, which together
> flow as a direct consequence from his nature. These rights
> and duties are universal and inviolable, and therefore alto-
> gether inalienable.[12]

Noteworthy, too, is the call to establish—by peaceful
means and "with the consent of all nations"[13]—a world
authority that will champion the universal common good
in the face of "problems which are world-wide in their
dimensions".[14] John writes:

> The common good of individual States is something that
> cannot be determined without reference to the human
> person, and the same is true of the common good of all
> States taken together. Hence the public authority of the
> world community must likewise have as its special aim
> the recognition, respect, safeguarding and promotion
> of the rights of the human person....
>   The special function of this universal authority must
> be to evaluate and find a solution to economic, social,
> political and cultural problems which affect the universal
> common good.[15]

[12] Ibid., no. 9.
[13] Ibid., no. 138.
[14] Ibid., no. 137.
[15] Ibid., nos. 139–40.

Pope John was diagnosed with stomach cancer in September 1962 and died on June 3, 1963. He remains one of the most popular popes ever. Perhaps because of this very popularity, says Hitchcock, many "myths" have come to be associated with his memory: the myth that he can be summed up simply as "pastoral"—he spent most of his career in the Church in administration and as a papal diplomat; that he was a simple soul—in fact, he was "intellectually and politically sophisticated"; that he was a liberal—but he mandated the teaching of Latin in seminaries at a time when many of them were phasing out Latin, while *The Journal of a Soul* gives us a picture of someone of "deep traditional piety" who, for example, directed that Saint Joseph be included in the Canon of the Mass in the face of the indifference of the Fathers of Vatican II.[16]

There is, however, nothing at all mythical about the fact that, as Paul Johnson remarks, Pope John showed "that a spiritual leader, whose sincerity is self-evident, can still make the world pause and think, at least for a time". He continues,

> In this sense, his work and example are encouraging: the world is not so exclusively dominated by material forces as we are accustomed to suppose.... John delivered his message of charity and hope not only to the collective multitudes but to many millions of individual human hearts, where it brought comfort and joy.[17]

Pope John XXIII was canonized by Pope Francis along with Pope John Paul II on April 27, 2014. After his death, a note was found attached to his will. It reads, "It is with a

---

[16] Hitchcock, *History of the Catholic Church*, 474.
[17] Johnson, *Pope John XXIII*, 243.

joyful heart that I renew wholly and fervently the profession of my Catholic, Apostolic and Roman faith."[18]

SAFEGUARDING AND EXPOUNDING A SACRED HERITAGE

We saw above that Pope John's mandate to the Second Vatican Council was essentially a call to devise ways of more effectively bringing Jesus Christ and his message to a world desperately in need of them. In his opening address to the council, he offered some guidelines for accomplishing what he had in mind. Following are further excerpts from this address, delivered in St. Peter's Basilica to twenty-four hundred assembled bishops from around the world on October 11, 1962.

The major interest of the Ecumenical Council is this: that the sacred heritage of Christian truth be safeguarded and expounded with greater efficacy.

That doctrine embraces the whole man, body and soul. It bids us live as pilgrims here on earth, as we journey onwards towards our heavenly homeland.

It demonstrates how we must conduct this mortal life of ours....

If this doctrine is to make its impact on the various spheres of human activity—in private, family and social life—then it is absolutely vital that the Church shall never for an instant lose sight of that sacred patrimony of truth inherited from the Fathers. But it is equally necessary for her to keep up to date with the changing conditions of the modern world, and of modern living, for these have opened up entirely new avenues for the Catholic apostolate....

[18] John XXIII, *Journal of a Soul*, 397.

From what We have said, the doctrinal role of this present Council is sufficiently clear....

Its intention is to give to the world the whole of that doctrine which, notwithstanding every difficulty and contradiction, has become the common heritage of mankind—to transmit it in all its purity, undiluted, undistorted.

It is a treasure of incalculable worth, not indeed coveted by all, but available to all men of good will.

And our duty is not just to guard this treasure, as though it were some museum-piece and we the curators, but earnestly and fearlessly to dedicate ourselves to the work that needs to be done in this modern age of ours, pursuing the path which the Church has followed for almost twenty centuries.

Nor are we here primarily to discuss certain fundamentals of Catholic doctrine, or to restate in greater detail the traditional teaching of the Fathers and of early and more recent theologians. We presume that these things are sufficiently well known and familiar to you all.

There was no need to call a council merely to hold discussions of that nature. What is needed at the present time is a new enthusiasm, a new joy and serenity of mind in the unreserved acceptance by all of the entire Christian faith, without forfeiting that accuracy and precision in its presentation which characterized the proceedings of the Council of Trent and the First Vatican Council. What is needed, and what everyone imbued with a truly Christian, Catholic and apostolic spirit craves today, is that this doctrine shall be more widely known, more deeply understood, and more penetrating in its effects on men's moral lives. What is needed is that this certain and immutable doctrine, to which the faithful owe obedience, be studied afresh and reformulated in contemporary terms. For this deposit of faith, or truths which are contained in our time-honored teaching is one thing; the manner in which these truths are set forth (with their meaning preserved intact) is something else....

Human ideologies change. Successive generations give rise to varying errors, and these often vanish as quickly as they came, like mist before the sun.

The Church has always opposed these errors, and often condemned them with utmost severity. Today, however, Christ's Bride prefers the balm of mercy to the arm of severity. She believes that present needs are best served by explaining more fully the purport of her doctrines, rather than by publishing condemnations....

Such, venerable brethren, is the aim of the Second Vatican Council. It musters the Church's best energies and studies with all earnestness how to have the message of salvation more readily welcomed by men. By that very fact it blazes a trail that leads toward that unity of the human race, which is so necessary if this earthly realm of ours is to conform to the realm of heaven, "whose king is truth, whose law is love, whose duration is eternity" (St. Augustine, *Ep.* 138, 3).[19]

[19] John XXIII, "Opening Address to the Council".

THE SECOND VATICAN COUNCIL

(1962–1965)

"Innovation in Continuity"

A conversation that took place not long ago among a small group of friends, all of them practicing Catholics, was typical of countless others since the Second Vatican Council. The talk had turned to Vatican II. Citing the many mishaps the Church had suffered since then, one man pinned the blame on the council. "What did we need a council for anyway?" he demanded, adding that the Church was doing quite well before Vatican II came along and turned everything upside down.

Another member of the group demurred. "I share many of the same concerns and reservations," he told the rest. "But imagine what the Church would be like today if there'd been no council. Do you really believe we could have stood pat on the Church of Pius XII—or the Church of John XXIII, for that matter—and expected people to take the Church seriously today? I don't."

An older man, a professor at a Catholic university, spoke up. With satisfaction, he reported that his children were all churchgoing Catholics—no small thing in this day and age. "But I'm pretty sure," he added, "that they wouldn't

Subtitle quote is from the Address of His Holiness Benedict XVI to the Roman Curia Offering Them His Christmas Greetings (December 22, 2005).

have stuck with it except for the council." His listeners were pleased for him and his children, but although some agreed with his assessment of Vatican II, others made it clear they definitely did not.

"I guess I'm just a pre-Vatican II Catholic," the one who had spoken first finally said with a shrug.

Few if any events in the recent history of the Catholic Church have called forth so many opinions so intensely held as Vatican Council II. One of the few things everyone agrees on is that the council was followed by a period of intense and sometimes raucous controversy and dissent, a dismaying number of noisy defections from the priesthood and religious life, numerous flagrant abuses in liturgical practice, and much else of a similarly alarming nature. Cambridge historian John Pollard expresses a widely held view in calling Vatican II "the great 'Pandora's box'" that opened the door to the emergence—not infrequently noisy and unsettling—of "forces for change" that had been suppressed in the Church since the early years of the century and Pius X's condemnation of Modernism. "The deep divisions on many issues between conservatives at the centre and liberals on the periphery, which had been largely hidden for several decades, had now broken the surface," Pollard writes.[1]

Catholic historian and writer Robert Royal is at pains to point out that the aberrations and destructive upheavals after Vatican II—the exodus from the priesthood and religious life, the calamitous falloff in new priestly and religious vocations, steep declines in Mass attendance in wealthy countries, the sudden visibility of Catholic theologians teaching in Catholic institutions who publicly denied

---

[1] John Pollard, *The Papacy in the Age of Totalitarianism, 1914–1958* (Oxford: Oxford University Press, 2014), 478.

the Church's doctrine on many moral questions as well as fundamentals of belief like the Real Presence, the divinity of Christ, and Christ's Resurrection—were not creatures of the council itself. But all, he adds, shared some connection with a fundamental misunderstanding of Vatican II that sets the "pastoral" in opposition to the "dogmatic".[2]

Significantly, Royal also takes issue with Karl Rahner, S.J., the German theologian who exerted a powerful influence on Vatican II as advisor to the German bishops, regarding his claim that the council was a "decisive break" with the previous history of the Church. "Rahner was right," he says, "in that the Council was a major turning point, but wrong in suggesting—as he did to some people—that the Church had undergone a transformation that simply broke with virtually the entirety of her previous existence." That many well-educated Catholics came to believe something of the kind really occurred at Vatican II, Royal says, is itself "a sign that something went strangely awry among the faithful and even among quite brilliant Catholic minds".[3]

But instead of dwelling on this argument, let's take a closer look at the Second Vatican Council as it was in fact. Here some history will help.

The First Vatican Council, formally convoked by Blessed Pius IX, was held between December 1869 and September 1870 with 754 bishops attending, over twice the number who had taken part in the Council of Trent three centuries earlier. The Orthodox churches had been invited to send observers but declined, while secular governments for the first time were not officially represented.

---

[2] Robert Royal, *A Deeper Vision: The Catholic Intellectual Tradition in the Twentieth Century* (San Francisco: Ignatius Press, 2015), 169–70.
[3] Ibid., 14.

Vatican I produced formal definitions (i.e., propositions declared to belong to the faith of the Church) of two dogmas: papal infallibility and papal primacy.

The council was not formally closed in 1870 but was only suspended as the bishops, now lacking the protection of a French garrison, hastened to leave Rome in the face of an impending assault by Italian nationalist troops bent on making the city the capital of the new, united Italy. For his part, Pius IX retired behind the Vatican walls and declared himself "the Prisoner of the Vatican", a state of affairs that would persist for the next fifty-nine years.

But what to do about Vatican I? The idea of reconvening it was seriously considered during the pontificates of both Pius XI and Pius XII. Matters suggested for discussion at such a gathering, identified by a study commissioned by Pius XI, included a dogmatic declaration covering the major elements of Catholic faith and a comprehensive treatment of the Church in her teaching, sanctifying, legislating, and judicial aspects and her relation to civil authority; while preliminary studies commissioned by Pope Pius XII in the latter years of his pontificate laid important groundwork for the council that was soon to take place.[4]

Two cardinals are said to have raised the idea of an ecumenical council with Cardinal Roncalli during the conclave of 1958 that elected him pope. But when Pope John XXIII (as he had become) disclosed his intention to convoke an ecumenical council, not everyone was persuaded it was a good idea. Some saw no particular need for a council: the Church was healthy and growing, and the pope, possessing infallibility and primacy, had all the authority he needed to handle any problem that might arise. Why complicate matters with an ecumenical council? Others

---

[4] Pollard, *Age of Totalitarianism*, 200–201, 478.

assumed that if there were to be a council, it would be short and to the point. Pope John himself supposed that Vatican II would require only a single session lasting a few weeks.

Despite the uncertainties and reservations, however, preparations moved ahead. An "ante-preparatory" commission established by Pope John invited the world's bishops to submit suggestions about topics. Responses ranged far and wide, but the 2,150 replies and 76.4 percent response rate suggested a high degree of interest on the part of the hierarchy. A preparatory commission established by Pope John in June 1960 now had more than enough to do, although the actual work of drafting documents was largely in the hands of the Roman Curia and Roman theologians. An important moment in the preparations was the pope's appointment of Father Augustin Bea, S.J., rector of the Pontifical Biblical Institute, to head a newly created Secretariat for Christian Unity. Father—soon, Cardinal— Bea threw himself enthusiastically into contacting other Christian bodies and arranging for non-Catholic observers at the council; and soon non-Catholic churchmen were trooping to Rome to meet with the pope.

Pope Saint John's historic opening address to the council on October 11, 1962, has been described and excerpted above. An eyewitness account of the council's opening by Father Ralph Wiltgen, S.V.D., serves to set the scene with a touch of color.[5] The cobblestones in St. Peter's

---

[5] There are many histories of the Second Vatican Council, written from a variety of ideological and theological perspectives. One of the first and still one of the best is *The Rhine Flows into the Tiber: A History of Vatican II*, by Father Wiltgen. Its first American edition was published by Hawthorn Books in New York, in March 1967. Perhaps because battle lines over the meaning of Vatican II had not yet been rigidly drawn then, the volume has the great merit of being a rigorously factual, highly informative account of *what actually happened* at Vatican Council II.

Square, he recalls, were wet and shiny that morning from overnight rain, but they dried quickly in bright sunshine beneath the feet of the crowd watching the Fathers of Vatican II assemble.

> The long white procession of bishops in miters and flowing copes seemed never to end. It came down the Royal Staircase, through the Bronze Door and halfway across the square. Then it turned abruptly to the right, mounted the steps and disappeared through the main entrance of St. Peter's....
>
> I stood on the front steps watching all 2400 Council Fathers pass by. These men for the most part were unknown outside their own dioceses. But some of them, because of what they would say, or do, were destined to live forever in the histories of the Council. Names like Frings, Ottaviani, Lienart, Meyer, Bea, Suenens, Leger, Maximos IV Saigh and Sigaud were just a few....
>
> Pope John finally appeared at the end of the procession, his face radiant with joy. Repeatedly he bowed to the crowd, giving his blessing, and gladly accepting their greetings in return.... At the main entrance to St. Peter's, his portable throne was lowered, and he proceeded down the long aisle on foot. The Council Fathers, now in their places in the huge Council hall ... applauded and cheered him as he passed.[6]

And then the twenty-first ecumenical council in the two-thousand-year history of the Catholic Church began.

The bishops taking part in Vatican II—some 2,860 of them attended some or all of it—came from every part of the world: Europe (39 percent), North America (14 percent), South America (18 percent), Central America (3 percent), Asia (12 percent), Africa (12 percent), and Oceania (2 percent). The council met in four two-month

---

[6] Ibid., 13.

sessions, October to December, from 1962 to 1965. Its general assemblies were held in St. Peter's Basilica. Counting preparatory work, it cost $7,250,000—about $2,535 per bishop (or $9 per bishop for each of its 281 days). Its tangible results were the sixteen documents adopted by overwhelming majorities of bishops (though often after long and occasionally heated debates and significant amendments) and approved by the pope. Totaling a little over 103,000 Latin words, these include four constitutions, nine decrees, and three declarations. The constitutions are the most important. They deal, respectively, with the Church (*Lumen Gentium*—the Light of the World, meaning Christ, not the Church), the Church in the modern world (*Gaudium et Spes*—Joy and Hope), the liturgy (*Sacrosanctum Concilium*—the Sacred Council), and divine revelation (*Dei Verbum*—the Word of God).

In theory, every bishop at the council was the equal of every other bishop, in the sense that all bishops were entitled to speak and each of them had one vote. But Vatican II was a human deliberative body, and as at any such gathering, so at the council some bishops naturally had more influence than others. Wiltgen says that, due to superior organization, this role was played at Vatican II largely by the bishops of northern Europe, especially those from German-speaking countries. The steps taken by this "European alliance" to hammer out consensus among its members and engage in coordinated action were, he writes, "very impressive, and it is to be regretted that all national and regional conferences [of bishops] did not work with the same intensity and purpose.... The Council would then have been less one-sided, and its achievements would truly have been the result of a worldwide theological effort."[7]

[7] Ibid., 79–80.

While the decrees and declarations of Vatican II, dealing with such matters as ecumenism, non-Christian reli-
gions (including a new and highly positive treatment of
the Catholic Church's relationship with Judaism), bishops
and priests, the renewal of religious life, the apostolate of
the laity (lay "ministries" did not make their appearance
until several years after Vatican II, although the council did
make provision for this development), religious liberty, and
missionary activity, are undoubtedly of much interest
and importance, the central documents of the council, as
noted, are these four constitutions: on the Church, the
Church in the modern world, the liturgy, and divine revelation. From a theological perspective, the various decrees
and declarations are often written as applications of principles set out in the constitutions and depend conceptually on them. Viewed against this background, three broad
themes stand out in the documents of Vatican II: prayer,
worship, and the life of the spirit; the nature, structures,
processes, and persons of the Church; and the Church's
relationship with the world. John W. O'Malley, S.J., in his
history of the council, also identifies three "issues-under-
the-issues" that he sees underlying the conciliar debates on
particular questions: when and to what extent change is
appropriate in the Church; the relationship in the Church
of "center to periphery"—that is, the proper way of distributing authority between the Holy See and the rest
of the Church; and the "style or model" according to
which that authority should be exercised and expressed.[8]

What follows makes no pretense to being a comprehensive account, but only provides the briefest of overviews of
the council's treatment of each of the three themes.

---

[8] John W. O'Malley, S.J., *What Happened at Vatican II* (Cambridge: Belknap
Press at Harvard University Press, 2008), 8–14.

1. Prayer, worship, and the life of the spirit

Sacrosanctum Concilium, the Constitution on the Sacred Liturgy, is obviously of central importance to any discussion of Vatican II and the life of the spirit. The long history of liturgical renewal preceding this document includes a lively movement for the reform of the liturgy dating back to the late nineteenth century, Pope Pius XII's groundbreaking 1947 encyclical *Mediator Dei*, various reforms subsequently introduced by that pope, and the adoption of innovations like the "dialogue Mass" involving congregational participation. These pre-Vatican II developments helped make adopting the liturgy constitution relatively easy for the bishops, and so, on December 4, 1963, *Sacrosanctum Concilium* became the first document voted by the council and promulgated by Pope Paul VI. Contrary to what many people suppose, the constitution does not abolish Latin in the Mass or call for such now-familiar features of liturgical celebration as lay ministers of Communion and female altar servers.

The first chapter of the constitution is its theological section. It stresses the presence and action of Christ in the Mass and the sacraments, which are also actions of the Church, declares the eucharistic liturgy to be the summit toward which all of the Church's activity is directed and the fount from which all of its power comes, and calls on pastors to do all they can to see to it that the faithful are able to take part in the liturgy "fully aware of what they are doing, actively engaged in the rite and enriched by it".[9]

---

[9] *Sacrosanctum Concilium*, no. 11. All Vatican II documents quoted in this chapter are taken from Austin Flannery, O.P., ed., *Vatican Council II*, vol. 1, *The Conciliar and Postconciliar Documents*, new rev. ed. (Northport, N.Y.: Costello, 1996).

The constitution then states the fundamental principles that must be kept always in view in anything done with the intention of renewing the liturgy.

> In the restoration and promotion of the sacred liturgy the full and active participation by all the people is the aim to be considered before all else....
>
> The liturgy is made up of unchangeable elements divinely instituted, and of elements subject to change. These latter not only may be changed but ought to be changed with the passage of time, if they have suffered from the intrusion of anything out of harmony with the inner nature of the liturgy or have become less suitable.... Both texts and rites should be drawn up so as to express more clearly the holy things which they signify. The Christian people ... should be able to understand them with ease and take part in them fully, actively, and as a community.[10]

But this, *Sacrosanctum Concilium* insists, is not to be understood as an invitation to unauthorized improvisation and experimentation. "Regulation of the sacred liturgy", the constitution specifies, belongs to the authority of the Holy See and, as relevant laws determine, of the local bishop, with episcopal conferences also possessing some authority, though within "defined limits". No one else, "not even a priest, may add, remove, or change anything in the liturgy on his own authority."[11]

Another pillar of Vatican II's view of the life of the spirit is its emphasis on Scripture. Cutting through old arguments, *Dei Verbum* (November 18, 1965) teaches that Sacred Tradition and Sacred Scripture comprise "a single

[10] Ibid., nos. 14, 21.
[11] Ibid., no. 22.

sacred deposit of the Word of God". The responsibility for providing the "authentic interpretation" of this body of revealed truth in either form belongs to "the living teaching office of the Church alone", it says.[12]

At the same time, and again setting aside disputes of the past, the constitution takes it for granted that Scripture scholarship, including the analysis of literary forms and historical studies, is a useful tool for understanding the Word of God; but it adds that whatever anyone might say by way of interpreting Scripture, everything is "ultimately subject to the judgment of the Church".[13] Quoting a famous saying of Saint Jerome—"Ignorance of the Scriptures is ignorance of Christ"[14]—it calls for prayerful reading and study of Sacred Scripture by all members of the Church, and expresses hope for "a new impulse of spiritual life" arising from it.[15]

2. The Church

Lumen Gentium, the Dogmatic Constitution on the Church (November 21, 1964), contains important teaching about the pope and the bishops and their relationship. Of special importance is what chapter 3 says about collegiality. The fundamental insight is that the bishops, as successors to the Apostles in union with the pope, make up a collegial body that shares in sanctifying, teaching, and governing the Church—both the local churches, which are the immediate responsibility of most bishops, and also the Church as a whole: "Together with their head, the Supreme Pontiff, and never apart from him, they

---

[12] *Dei Verbum*, no. 10.

[13] Ibid., no. 12.

[14] Ibid., no. 25, quoting Saint Jerome, *Commentary on Isaiah*, Prol.: PL 24, 17.

[15] Ibid., no. 26.

[the bishops] have supreme and full authority over the universal Church."[16]

This is the basis for post–Vatican II innovations like the Synod of Bishops, whose structure, competence, and mode of operation remain in flux even now, and the decision-making process called "synodality". After Pope Paul VI at the start of the council's fourth and final session announced the creation of the synod, as a new, permanent institutional embodiment of the collegial principle, Father Joseph Ratzinger (the future Pope Benedict XVI) wrote that the synod was to be something like a "permanent council in miniature".[17] Up to this time, however, it has functioned in a purely advisory capacity in relation to the pope.

Vatican II's attention to the spiritual life of laypeople, present in its treatment of both the liturgy and the Bible, reaches a high point in *Lumen Gentium*. Chapter 4 of the constitution is devoted entirely to the laity, while chapter 5, "The Call to Holiness", insists that sanctity is for everyone:

> It is therefore quite clear that all Christians in any state or walk of life are called to the fullness of Christian life and to the perfection of love, and by this holiness a more human manner of life is fostered also in earthly society.... The forms and tasks of life are many but holiness is one.[18]

---

[16] *Lumen Gentium*, no. 22.

[17] Joseph Ratzinger, *Theological Highlights of Vatican II* (New York/Mahwah, N.J.: Paulist Press, 1966), 204. Originally published in Germany as four separate booklets, each appearing after one of the sessions of the council, the book remains an interesting contemporary commentary on Vatican II. Father Ratzinger was present at the council as theological peritus to Joseph Cardinal Frings of Cologne, one of the council's most important figures, and was an active member of the group of theologians who did so much to shape the thinking of Vatican II.

[18] *Lumen Gentium*, nos. 40–41.

The council goes on to speak specifically of married couples and parents, widows and single people, workers, the poor, and the sick.

In a sense, this was not new: the Church has always offered laypeople the means of becoming saints—prayer, the sacraments, generous service of others—and has encouraged their use. Yet all too often, and for many centuries, the working assumption appeared to be that it was unreasonable to expect most lay Catholics to rise much beyond spiritual minimalism. Before Vatican II, however, some new groups had begun to challenge this assumption and to encourage even the "ordinary" laity to seek sanctity. Now this message was repeated and endorsed authoritatively by an ecumenical council: "All Christians, in the conditions and circumstances of their life and through all these, will sanctify themselves more and more if they receive all things with faith."[19]

3. The Church and the world

Vatican II also broke new ground by speaking of the world outside the Church in its Pastoral Constitution on the Church in the Modern World, *Gaudium et Spes* (December 7, 1965). Here, one might say, the council took to heart its own admonition that separating faith from life is "one of the gravest errors of our time"[20] and stands badly in need of correcting.

In the sixty years before Vatican II, of course, the popes of the twentieth century had spoken often of the secular world's errors and problems. Usually, however, this was done in a judgmental and prescriptive manner, and the voice of the Church repeatedly went unheeded.

[19] Ibid., no. 41.
[20] *Gaudium et Spes*, no. 43.

(In fairness, one must ask how else except judgmentally Benedict XV should have spoken about the deadly folly of World War I or Pius XI about the mad semireligious ideology of blood and soil that was part and parcel of Nazism.)

Now, in any case, without giving up the making of judgments and the offering of prescriptions, the council Fathers consciously, perhaps even a bit self-consciously, sought to address the world in an open, dialogical manner, which O'Malley describes admiringly as "a style less unilateral in its decision-making, a style committed to fair play and to working with persons and institutions outside the Catholic community".[21] The famous words with which *Gaudium et Spes* begins are exemplary: "The joy and hope, the grief and anguish of the men of our time, especially those who are poor or afflicted in any way, are the joy and hope, the grief and anguish of the followers of Christ as well. Nothing that is genuinely human fails to find an echo in their hearts."[22]

The results, both at the time and now, were mixed.

On the one hand, *Gaudium et Spes* was an earnest and sometimes successful attempt by the council to engage the new secular realities of the day. On the other hand, critics accuse the pastoral constitution of taking a naively optimistic view of the human condition in the late twentieth century. "It is an open question," Joseph Ratzinger writes, "whether the final text really succeeded in finding an adequate form for addressing the world. But the effort alone must be rated an important accomplishment and a step in the right direction."[23]

[21] O'Malley, *What Happened at Vatican II*, 308.
[22] *Gaudium et Spes*, no. 1.
[23] Ratzinger, *Theological Highlights*, 225.

To its credit, the council did not give facile answers to problems relating to the many large issues it addressed—marriage and the family, faith and culture, economic and social life, work and leisure, politics and public life, and much else. This was notably true—and a source of frustration for some—where modern warfare and the threat of nuclear war were concerned. Speaking twenty years after the first atomic bombs fell on Hiroshima and Nagasaki, the council condemned "indiscriminate destruction of whole cities or vast areas" such as would occur in a largescale use of nuclear weapons. But *Gaudium et Spes*, appearing in the Cold War years, left it at that, stopping short of saying no to any use whatsoever of nuclear weapons and to nuclear deterrence.[24] This approach, Father Ratzinger says, reflected an "emergency morality" in the face of the "radical unrighteousness" tragically characteristic of the modern world.[25]

In the long run, however, the most important contribution of *Gaudium et Spes* may be its insistence on the dignity of the human person as seen in the light of a christological anthropology. Central to the vision of Vatican II is a passage of the pastoral constitution that is arguably the single most important statement of the entire council:

> Christ the Lord, Christ the new Adam, in the very revelation of the mystery of the Father and of his love, fully reveals man to himself and brings to light his most high calling.[26]

Hardly less important is what the council says about the meaning and value of human life in the temporal order.

---

[24] For the council's treatment of these matters, see *Gaudium et Spes*, no. 80.
[25] Ratzinger, *Theological Highlights*, 243.
[26] *Gaudium et Spes*, no. 22.

Its· significance can only be fully appreciated in the light of the long history of Christian ascetical thinking along *contemptus mundi* lines: the world is a place of temptation and trial—a vale of tears where even the highest accomplishments of mankind have no lasting value and the only truly Christian response is to shun the world and look to the next life. Against that background, how different is this from *Gaudium et Spes*:

> The form of this world, distorted by sin, is passing away and we are taught that God is preparing a new dwelling and a new earth in which righteousness dwells, whose happiness will fill and surpass all the desires of peace arising in the hearts of men....
>
> Far from diminishing our concern to develop this earth, the expectancy of a new earth should spur us on, for it is here that the body of a new human family grows, foreshadowing in some way the age which is to come. That is why, although we must be careful to distinguish earthy progress clearly from the increase of the kingdom of Christ, such progress is of vital concern to the kingdom of God, insofar as it can contribute to the better ordering of human society.
>
> When we have spread on earth the fruits of our nature and our enterprise—human dignity, brotherly communion, and freedom—according to the command of the Lord and in his Spirit, we will find them once again, cleansed this time from the stain of sin, illuminated and transfigured, when Christ presents to his Father an eternal and universal kingdom "of truth and life, a kingdom of holiness and grace, a kingdom of justice, love and peace" [Preface for the Feast of Christ the King]. Here on earth the kingdom is mysteriously present; when the Lord comes it will enter into its perfection.[27]

[27] Ibid., no. 39.

Contempt for the world is not Christianity's final word on the temporal order. For the good we do here and now will last, and in this way we do our part in building up the Kingdom of God.

The years since Vatican II have witnessed a continuing argument between proponents of two radically opposed interpretations of the council. Call them, for want of better names, the "textualists" and the "spirit of Vatican II" people.

Pope Benedict XVI provided a lucid account of this debate in an important address on December 22, 2005, to the Roman Curia. He began with a question: "Why has the implementation of the Council, in large parts of the Church, thus far been so difficult?" His answer: "Two contrary hermeneutics came face to face and quarrelled with each other. One caused confusion, the other, silently but more and more visibly, bore and is bearing fruit."

Benedict continued:

On the one hand, there is an interpretation that I would call "a hermeneutic of discontinuity and rupture"; it has frequently availed itself of the sympathies of the mass media, and also one trend of modern theology. On the other, there is the "hermeneutic of reform", of renewal in the continuity of one subject-Church which the Lord has given to us. She is a subject which increases in time and develops, yet always remaining the same, the one subject of the journeying People of God.

The hermeneutic of discontinuity risks ending in a split between the pre-conciliar Church and the post-conciliar Church. It asserts that the texts of the Council as such do not yet express the true spirit of the Council. It claims that they are the result of compromises in which, to reach unanimity, it was found necessary to keep and reconfirm many old things that are now pointless. However, the true spirit of the Council is not to be found in these compromises but instead in the impulses toward the new that are contained in the texts.

Then the pope points with evident approval to a way of interpreting the Second Vatican Council that he calls the way of reform.

> The hermeneutic of discontinuity is countered by the hermeneutic of reform, as it was presented first by Pope John XXIII in his Speech inaugurating the Council on 11 October 1962 and later by Pope Paul VI in his Discourse for the Council's conclusion on 7 December 1965.
>
> Here I shall cite only John XXIII's well-known words, which unequivocally express this hermeneutic when he says that the Council "wishes to transmit the doctrine, pure and integral, without any attenuation or distortion". And he continues: "Our duty is not only to guard this precious treasure, as if we were concerned only with antiquity, but to dedicate ourselves with an earnest will and without fear to that work which our era demands of us" (*The Documents of Vatican II*, Walter M. Abbott, S.J., p. 715).

Pope Benedict goes on to insist that genuine reform—which he says is the product of "innovation in continuity"—is found "precisely in this combination of continuity and discontinuity at different levels". Where reform has been undertaken in this spirit, he says, "new life developed and new fruit ripened."[28]

VATICAN II'S CHRISTOLOGICAL ANTHROPOLOGY

In his important address on the proper understanding of Vatican II, Pope Benedict underlines the council's

---

[28] Address Offering His Christmas Greetings.

christological understanding of the human person, calling it a needed contribution to "the great dispute about man which marks the modern epoch".[29] The excerpts that follow, from chapter 1 of *Gaudium et Spes* ("The Dignity of the Human Person"), indicate consequences that the council saw flowing from this vision of human dignity.

[Today] there is a growing awareness of the sublime dignity of the human person, who stands above all things and whose rights and duties are universal and inviolable. He ought, therefore, to have ready access to all that is necessary for living a genuinely human life: for example, food, clothing, housing, the right freely to choose his state of life and set up a family, the right to education, work, to his good name, to respect, to proper knowledge, the right to act according to the dictates of conscience and to safeguard his privacy, and rightful freedom even in matters of religion....

The varieties of crime [against the human person] are numerous: all offenses against life itself, such as murder, genocide, abortion, euthanasia and willful suicide; all violations of the integrity of the human person, such as mutilation, physical and mental torture, undue psychological pressures; all offenses against human dignity, such as subhuman living conditions, arbitrary imprisonment, deportation, slavery, prostitution, the selling of women and children, degrading working conditions where men are treated as mere tools for profit rather than free and responsible persons: all these and the like are criminal: they poison civilization; and they debase the perpetrators more than the victims and militate against the honor of the creator....

All men are endowed with a rational soul and are created in God's image; they have the same nature and origin and, being redeemed by Christ, they enjoy the same divine calling and destiny; there is here a basic equality between all men and it must be given ever greater recognition.

[29] Ibid.

Undoubtedly not all men are alike as regards physical capacity and intellectual and moral powers. But forms of social or cultural discrimination in basic personal rights on the grounds of sex, race, color, social conditions, language or religion, must be curbed and eradicated as incompatible with God's design. It is regrettable that these basic rights are not yet being respected everywhere, as is the case with women who are denied the chance freely to choose a husband, or a state of life, or to have access to the same educational and cultural benefits as are available to men.

Furthermore, while there are rightful differences between people, their equal dignity as persons demands that we strive for fairer and more humane conditions. Excessive economic and social disparity between individuals and people of the one human race is a source of scandal and militates against social justice, equity, human dignity, as well as social and international peace.[30]

[30] *Gaudium et Spes*, nos. 26–27, 29.

POPE SAINT PAUL VI

(June 21, 1963–August 6, 1978)

"Am I Hamlet or Don Quixote?"

In his popular history of the papacy, *Saints and Sinners*, Eamon Duffy declares that no pope since Saint Gregory the Great has faced "so daunting a task" as Saint Paul VI.[1] That is a large claim certainly but a defensible one. Gregory, pope from 590 to 604, had to cope with barbarian invasions and the breakdown of the Roman Empire. Paul VI, in the midst of cultural revolution in society and the Church, was called upon to confront the neo-barbarians of postconciliar Catholicism who, acting in what they liked to call the "spirit" of the Second Vatican Council, claimed to discern—while also seeking to bring about—a definitive rupture separating the Church as it had been before Vatican II and the Church as they wanted it to be after the council.

It was this mindset as much as any other that in the end frustrated so many of Pope Paul's hopes for the Church. Yet some such clash appears to have been inevitable in an era that celebrated sexual liberation and self-indulgence while the pope was upholding the traditional ethos in his

The subtitle quote is by Paul VI, in Eamon Duffy, *Saints and Sinners: A History of the Popes* (New Haven, Conn.: Yale University Press, 2006), 368.

[1] Ibid., 363.

encyclical *Humanae Vitae*—and paying a high price for having done that.

Unquestionably, too, he suffered in the public eye by comparison with his charismatic predecessor. If Pope John XXIII's image were to be summed up in a word, that word might be "charming". The word for Paul would be "dutiful". And although doing one's duty has much to recommend it, it can't hold a candle to charm in a competition for popularity where image is nine-tenths of the game.

Dogging Paul, too, was his hesitancy in making hard decisions, which caused some to liken him (and even moved him to liken himself) to Shakespeare's indecisive prince of Denmark, Hamlet. Pope John had given the appearance of deciding things without fretting too much, as in his seemingly snap decision to convoke an ecumenical council. In Paul's case, decision-making came harder, perhaps because his keen intelligence caused him to see more potential consequences of any particular course of action than most people ordinarily do, or perhaps because of the internal tension between his own progressive and conservative leanings. Duffy calls him "a complex man, affectionate, capable of deep and enduring friendships, yet reserved, prone to fits of depression, easily hurt". Strongly committed to the ecumenical council as an instrument for setting directions for the Church, he believed no less strongly in papal primacy as he had seen it exercised years before by Pius XI and Pius XII. In any case, for whatever reason or combination of reasons, the tensions of his position gradually wore him down. "His last years," Duffy concludes, "were a sort of slow crucifixion for him."[2]

Giovanni Battista Montini was born on September 26, 1897, in Concesio, a town near the city of Brescia in the

---

[2] Ibid., 368.

north of Italy. His father, Giorgio, was a lawyer, newspaper editor, and leader in Catholic Action who served in parliament. The shy, bookish young man entered the seminary in 1916, was ordained in 1920, and then pursued graduate studies in Rome at the Gregorian University, La Sapienza University, and, by invitation, at the Accademia dei Nobili Ecclesiastici, the training school for clerics preparing for the papal diplomatic service.

In 1922 he joined the staff of the Vatican Secretariat of State, where he worked with other young priests who included Alfredo Ottaviani, a future prefect of the Holy Office, and Francis Spellman of Boston, a future archbishop of New York. After serving briefly at the nunciature in Warsaw, he returned to the secretariat in Rome while also teaching diplomatic history at the Accademia.

In 1937 he was named substitute (i.e., assistant) secretary of state under Eugenio Cardinal Pacelli. When Cardinal Pacelli became Pope Pius XII two years later, he continued in that position, and for the decade and a half that followed functioned as a top official of the Secretariat of State while also serving in effect as private secretary of the pope, whom he deeply admired. Within the Vatican, John Pollard writes, he represented the "more 'liberal,' more open tendency".[3] During World War II he headed the Vatican office that assisted prisoners of war and refugees— eventually it handled nearly ten million requests for help— and coordinated efforts to shelter Jews and other refugees in the city's parishes, convents, and church schools as well as at the papal summer residence at Castel Gandolfo, where some fifteen thousand lived.

In November 1954, after a falling-out with the pope apparently occasioned by his comparatively liberal leanings,

[3] John Pollard, *The Papacy in the Age of Totalitarianism 1914–1958* (Oxford: Oxford University Press, 2014), 298.

Pius XII named him archbishop of the giant Archdiocese of Milan. Only in December 1958 did a new pope, John XXIII, elevate him to the College of Cardinals.

Upon learning of Pope John's plan to convene an ecumenical council, he is said to have remarked privately that John was stirring up a hornets' nest. As time passed, however, he became a supporter of the council and played an active role at its first session in 1962. On June 21, 1963, at the conclave following John XXIII's death, Cardinal Montini was elected to succeed him—apparently on the fifth ballot. One of his first acts was to declare that the ecumenical council would continue.

Truly, his credentials for the papacy were peerless. From his years as a close collaborator of Pius XII, he possessed unsurpassed knowledge of the structures and personalities of the Church. His time in Milan had given him hands-on experience in governing one of the world's premier sees. Now he seemed poised for a pontificate of historic significance.

And undoubtedly it did have its high points: a historic meeting in Jerusalem in January 1964 with Orthodoxy's Ecumenical Patriarch Athenagoras I, followed by further steps toward healing the millennium-old split between Catholicism and the Orthodox churches; his dramatic October 1965 visit to the United Nations, where he electrified the world with a moving address in which he cried out, "No more war"; and the triumphant conclusion of the ecumenical council in December 1965 after he had guided it through the final three of its sometimes turbulent and conflicted sessions to an ending that seemed to promise a bright future for the Church.

Pope Paul also published in 1967 (March 26) an important social encyclical, *Populorum Progressio* (The Progress of Peoples), aligning the Church with the concerns of developing nations. The encyclical pointed to a threefold duty of wealthy nations, summed up as mutual solidarity ("the aid that the richer nations must give to developing nations"), social justice ("the rectification of trade relations between strong and weak nations"), and universal charity ("the effort to build a more humane world community, where all can give and receive, and where the progress of some is not bought at the expense of others").[4] As for the ultimate goal of development, Pope Paul left no doubt about that: "Organized programs designed to increase productivity should have but one aim: to serve human nature." Spelling out his personalist vision, he wrote:

> They [organized programs of development] should reduce inequities, eliminate discrimination, free men from the bonds of servitude, and thus give them the capacity, in the sphere of temporal realities, to improve their lot, to further their moral growth and to develop their spiritual endowments.... The mistakes of those who led the way should help those now on the road to development to avoid certain dangers. The reign of technology—technocracy, as it is called—can cause as much harm to the world of tomorrow as liberalism did to the world of yesteryear. Economics and technology are meaningless if they do not benefit man, for it is he they are to serve. Man is truly human only if he is the master of his own actions and the judge of their worth, only if he is the architect of his own progress. He must act according to his God-given nature, freely accepting its potentials and its claims upon him.[5]

Almost from the start of the pontificate, however, Paul seems to have had a sense of foreboding concerning what

---

[4] *Populorum Progressio*, no. 44.
[5] Ibid., no. 34.

lay ahead. "The post is unique," he wrote privately of the papacy soon after his election. "I was solitary before, but now my solitariness becomes complex and awesome.... My duty is to plan, decide, assume every responsibility for guiding others.... And so suffer alone."[6]

His greatest trial, as events were to show, concerned the issue of contraception. By the time he came to office, a commission that Pope John had established to prepare for Vatican participation in a UN conference on population had long since broadened its mandate and been engaged for several years in discussing the Church's teaching on artificial birth control. Would the Church accept the Pill? Could it allow other methods of contraception as well? With encouragement from people eager for change, the impression had started to spread that a major change in the Church's position might be in the works. Meanwhile Pope Paul studied the arguments and prayed. Too long, some said. For as time passed, what had only been speculation hardened into near certainty that change was coming.[7]

Then, on July 25, 1968, the encyclical *Humanae Vitae* appeared. Repeating the condemnation of all forms of contraception that had long been part of the Church's teaching, it declared: "Each and every marital act must of necessity retain its intrinsic relationship to the procreation of human life."[8]

---

[6] Quoted in Duffy, *Saints and Sinners*, 367.

[7] There is a careful account of the Commission on Population, Family, and Birth Rate and its work by the American ethicist and moral theologian Germain Grisez on his website, *The Way of the Lord Jesus* (http://twotlj.org /grisez_collaborators.html). Grisez was enlisted by Father John C. Ford, S.J., a moral theologian and member of the commission who defended the Church's traditional teaching on contraception, to assist him in developing material for the commission in its latter stages. See "About John C. Ford, S.J.", *The Way of the Lord Jesus*, accessed July 26, 2019, www.twotlj.org/Ford.html.

[8] *Humanae Vitae*, no. 11.

This papal document has often been called prophetic,[9] and it is easy to see why. In setting out the Church's teaching, Paul VI challenged a dogma of the midcentury revolution in sexual mores by then in full swing in the West. In doing so, he pointed to "marital infidelity and a general lowering of moral standards" as likely consequences of approving artificial contraception, though ones for which Catholics who called for the approval of contraception were hardly likely to accept responsibility.[10]

And, in a remarkable passage that stands as a kind of apologia for *Humanae Vitae* and for himself as its author, Paul acknowledged that the encyclical would encounter resistance—the "clamorous outcry" already typically raised against the Church whenever it engaged in moral teaching, but now "intensified" by the media. But since the Church did not make the moral law, he pointed out, it could not be its arbiter, only its guardian and interpreter. Moreover, "in preserving intact the whole moral law of marriage, the Church is convinced that she is contributing to the creation of a truly human civilization. She urges man not to betray his personal responsibilities by putting all his faith in technical expedients. In this way she defends the dignity of husband and wife."[11]

Time and events have vindicated Pope Paul, but immediate reactions to the encyclical were largely negative. Looking back, it is clear that *Humanae Vitae* could hardly have come at a worse time. In 1968 a cultural—and

---

[9] See, for example, Mary Eberstadt, "The Prophetic Power of Humanae Vitae", *First Things*, April 2018, https://www.firstthings.com/article/2018/04/the-prophetic-power-of-humanae-vitae. Eberstadt writes: "The most globally reviled and widely misunderstood document of the last half century is also the most prophetic and explanatory of our time."

[10] *Humanae Vitae*, no. 17.

[11] Ibid., no. 18.

sexual—revolution was well underway in the United States and other countries, creating a tidal wave of rebellion that threatened to sweep aside whatever smacked of authority and tradition. Antiauthority sentiment was rising in the United States in opposition to the American role in Vietnam. Within the Church, the turmoil of the years immediately after the ecumenical council was in full swing, while the ill-defined "spirit of Vatican II" led many to believe that old beliefs and values could, and no doubt should, be tossed aside. That obviously included the teaching against artificial birth control.

Widespread dissent by Catholic theologians greeted *Humanae Vitae*, some of it obviously orchestrated—for example, a full-page ad with numerous signers opposing the encyclical that appeared in the *New York Times* just a day after the document's publication. Even some bishops and bishops' conferences waffled or looked for loopholes. These included the hierarchies of France, the Netherlands, Canada, Germany, Austria, and Scandinavia. The bishops of the United States, speaking via a collective pastoral letter entitled *Human Life in Our Day*, supported the encyclical ("a defense of life and of love ... prophetic and in its world-view providential"), but somewhat spoiled the effect of their statement by including a section headed "Norms of Licit Theological Dissent" that provided guidelines for rejecting the encyclical.[12] This was arguably appropriate to a graduate seminar where proponents of differing points of view set out their positions in well-reasoned, genteel disputation; but the real

[12] *Human Life in Our Day*, Pastoral Letter by the National Conference of Catholic Bishops (November 15, 1968). The text used here is from Priests for Life, https://www.priestsforlife.org/magisterium/bishops/68-11-15human lifeinourdaynccb.htm.

world of 1968 dissent from *Humanae Vitae* took place in news conferences, media interviews, and opinion pieces written for newspapers and popular journals.

Meanwhile other developments added to the impression that all was not well with the Church. Even before the ecumenical council ended, priests and nuns had begun leaving the priesthood and religious life in large numbers, and now the exodus swelled. New vocations to the clerical state and consecrated life dropped precipitously. Conflict and dissent spread from the question of contraception to fundamental tenets of faith. Changes in the liturgy far beyond anything envisaged by Vatican II alienated many. So did truly bizarre liturgical experiments, notoriously including Masses involving balloons and clowns. And, over on the far right of the Catholic spectrum, even legitimate innovations sometimes drew the wrath of extreme conservatives like Evelyn Waugh, who in his last letter wrote: "Before Pope John and his Council—they destroyed the beauty of the liturgy. I have not yet soaked myself in petrol and gone up in flames, but I now cling to the Faith doggedly without joy."[13] And, of course, not everyone clung to the faith, whether doggedly or not.

The burden of all this came to rest finally on the shoulders of a conscientious, sensitive man who, looking from the window of his apartment overlooking St. Peter's Square, saw a Church and a world that sometimes seemed to have lost their minds. In a homily preached on June 29, 1972, the feast of Saints Peter and Paul, he suggested a startling explanation for what was happening. "Through some fissure," he said, "the smoke of Satan has entered the temple of God"—something diabolical had come on

---

[13] Quoted in Robert Royal, *A Deeper Vision: The Catholic Intellectual Tradition in the Twentieth Century* (San Francisco: Ignatius Press, 2015), 540.

the scene "to disturb, to suffocate the fruits of the ecumen-ical council".[14]

The last decade of Paul VI's pontificate was not a happy time, either for him or for the Church at large. Yet it still had its bright spots. One of the brightest was the publica-tion on December 8, 1975, of Paul VI's apostolic exhorta-tion on evangelization, *Evangelii Nuntiandi*. The opening passage of this farsighted document sums up Paul's own program as visible head of the Church: "There is no doubt that the effort to proclaim the Gospel to the people of today, who are buoyed up by hope but at the same time oppressed by fear and distress, is a service rendered to the Christian community and also to the whole of human-ity."[15] *Evangelii Nuntiandi* played a central role in launch-ing and providing intellectual and spiritual guidance for the renewed—though still largely unrealized—emphasis on Catholic evangelization in the years since it first appeared. (See excerpts below.)

Pope Paul's last days bordered on tragedy. Leftist radi-cals kidnapped his old friend Aldo Moro, a leader of Ita-ly's Christian Democratic Party, and brutally murdered him despite Paul's public plea for his release. Presiding at Moro's funeral in the Archbasilica of St. John Lateran, the cathedral of the bishop of Rome, was his last public act. While resting at Castel Gandolfo, the ailing pope suffered a massive heart attack. He died on August 6, 1978. In private notes he once wrote: "Am I Hamlet or Don Quixote?"[16] The answer may be, a bit of both. He was canonized by Pope Francis on October 14, 2018.

Paul VI is remembered by some people today as a leader who erred by pressing excessively liberal changes in the

[14] Ibid., 114.
[15] *Evangelii Nuntiandi*, no. 1.
[16] Quoted in Duffy, *Saints and Sinners*, 368.

Church and by others as one whose glaring failure was to stand on the side of tradition in *Humanae Vitae*. Speaking of the great project laid out by the Second Vatican Council, James Hitchcock pronounces what is by implication a surprisingly harsh judgment on this pope: "Ultimately, it was left to Paul's successors to begin the process of authentic renewal."[17] But others believe he made a brave beginning in exceedingly difficult times.

EVANGELIZING A SECULARIZED WORLD

Evangelii Nuntiandi was Pope Paul's response to the Third Ordinary General Assembly of the Synod of Bishops that had taken place a year earlier on the theme of evangelization (1974). The document is long, complex, and (if it still be possible in these cynical times to use the word without irony) inspiring. In the excerpts that follow, Paul discusses circumstances that presented special challenges to the Church's efforts to evangelize in his day—and continue to do that now.

From the spiritual point of view, the modern world seems to be forever immersed in what a modern author has termed "the drama of atheistic humanism."[18]

On the one hand one is forced to note in the very heart of this contemporary world the phenomenon which is becoming almost its most striking characteristic: secularism ... a concept of the world according to which the latter is self-explanatory, without any need for recourse to God....

[17] James Hitchcock, *History of the Catholic Church* (San Francisco: Ignatius Press, 2012), 508.

[18] The title of a well-known 1945 book by Henri de Lubac, S.J.

New forms of atheism seem to flow from it: a man centered atheism, no longer abstract and metaphysical but pragmatic, systematic and militant. Hand in hand with this atheistic secularism, we are daily faced, under the most diverse forms, with a consumer society, the pursuit of pleasure set up as the supreme value, a desire for power and domination, and discrimination of every kind: the inhuman tendencies of this "humanism."

In this same modern world, on the other hand, and this is a paradox, one cannot deny the existence of real steppingstones to Christianity, and of evangelical values at least in the form of a sense of emptiness or nostalgia. It would not be an exaggeration to say that there exists a powerful and tragic appeal to be evangelized.

The second sphere is that of those who do not practice. Today there is a very large number of baptized people who for the most part have not formally renounced their Baptism but who are entirely indifferent to it and not living in accordance with it.... The non-practicing Christians of today, more so than those of previous periods, seek to explain and justify their position in the name of an interior religion, of personal independence or authenticity.

Thus we have atheists and unbelievers on the one side and those who do not practice on the other, and both groups put up a considerable resistance to evangelization. The resistance of the former takes the form of a certain refusal and an inability to grasp the new order of things, the new meaning of the world, of life and of history; such is not possible if one does not start from a divine absolute. The resistance of the second group takes the form of inertia and the slightly hostile attitude of the person ... who claims to know it all and to have tried it all and who no longer believes it....

The power of evangelization will find itself considerably diminished if those who proclaim the Gospel are divided among themselves in all sorts of ways. Is this not perhaps one of the great sicknesses of evangelization today? Indeed, if the Gospel that we proclaim is seen to be rent by doctrinal disputes, ideological polarizations or mutual condemnations among Christians, at the mercy of the latter's differing views on Christ and the Church and even because of their different concepts of society and human institutions, how can those to whom we address our preaching fail to be disturbed, disoriented, even scandalized?

The Lord's spiritual testament tells us that unity among His followers is not only the proof that we are His but also the proof that He is sent by the Father. It is the test of the credibility of Christians and of Christ Himself. As evangelizers, we must offer Christ's faithful not the image of people divided and separated by unedifying quarrels, but the image of people who are mature in faith and capable of finding a meeting-point beyond the real tensions, thanks to a shared, sincere and disinterested search for truth. Yes, the destiny of evangelization is certainly bound up with the witness of unity given by the Church. This is a source of responsibility and also of comfort.[19]

---

[19] *Evangelium Nuntiandi*, nos. 55–56, 77.

POPE JOHN PAUL I

(August 26–September 28, 1978)

The Smiling Pope

When the cardinals gathered to choose a successor to Pope Paul VI, they wanted a smiling pope—a pontiff who would dispel the gloom that had darkened the closing years of the pontificate of Pope Paul. In the person of Albino Cardinal Luciani, patriarch of Venice, they got one. He took the name John Paul I.

In contrast with his cerebral, sensitive predecessor, Cardinal Luciani was considered to be a simple, good-humored bishop with a style more nearly that of John XXIII than Paul VI. The new pontiff adopted the names of his two immediate predecessors as a sign of respect for both and especially of his commitment to continue the implementation of the ecumenical council that John had begun and Paul had brought to a successful conclusion. As his papal motto he took the same motto he had taken on becoming a bishop—*Humilitas*.

Unfortunately, besides getting a pope with a great smile and a winning manner, the cardinals who elected him, apparently on the third or fourth ballot of the conclave's first day, August 26, unknowingly chose a man with health issues that a mere thirty-three days later would cause his death, making his pontificate one of the shortest ever. Today Pope John Paul is remembered largely for his famous smile. What he might have done as pope obviously is unknown.

Born October 17, 1912, in Forno di Canale (now, Canale d'Agordo), a village in northern Italy near Belluno, Albino Luciani was the oldest of four children in a family of very modest means.[1] His father was a bricklayer who often went to Switzerland to find work. When his son announced that he wanted to enter the seminary, the elder Luciani is said to have replied, "I hope that when you become a priest you will be on the side of the workers."[2]

Ordained in 1935, he became a professor and vice-rector of Belluno's seminary in 1937. Later he served as chancellor and then vicar general of the diocese. Excused from the requirement that he reside in Rome, he studied theology at the Gregorian University and received a doctorate in theology in 1947. Having been responsible for catechesis in connection with a eucharistic congress in Belluno in 1949, he drew on that experience to write *Catechetica in Briciole* (*Crumbs from the Catechism*), a book about teaching the faith to simple people. Named bishop of Vittorio Veneto in December 1958 by Pope John XXIII, he took part in all four sessions of the Second Vatican Council, though without being one of the council's leading lights. He also was an active member of the Italian bishops' conference, serving on its doctrinal committee and, from 1972 to 1975, as conference vice president.[3]

---

[1] There does not appear to be any full-scale biography of Pope John Paul in English. Biographical information here is drawn from several sources as cited in the footnotes and his moral teaching from J. N. D. Kelly's *The Oxford Dictionary of Popes* (Oxford: Oxford University Press, 1986), 325–26.

[2] "The Life of Albino Luciani", Pope John Paul I Association, March 17, 2015, jpicentenary.org.

[3] "Highlights of the Life of His Holiness John Paul I", Vatican.va, accessed November 21, 2019.

On December 15, 1969, Pope Paul named him patriarch of Venice, a position that had already been held twice in the twentieth century by future popes, both of them now canonized saints: Pius X, who served in Venice from 1893 to 1903, and John XXIII, 1953 to 1958. It seems likely that when Bishop Luciani became patriarch in 1969, not many people saw the unassuming new holder of the office as potentially the third to make the transition from Venice to the papacy before the century was out.

In 1971 Paul VI selected him to attend the world Synod of Bishops held in October of that year. There he delivered an intervention in which he proposed that wealthy countries give 1 percent of their annual incomes to poor ones—"not as alms but as something that is owed" them as a consequence of their exploitation by rich nations.[4] In 1973 Pope Paul elevated him to the College of Cardinals.

During his pre-papal years, Cardinal Luciani addressed many religious and social issues.

He sold a gold cross given him by Pope John XXIII and used the money to help children with disabilities while encouraging his priests to practice similar charity.[5] He established family counseling clinics to help poor people deal with marital and financial problems. He opposed the idea of worker priests (priests who would hold regular jobs alongside factory workers, thereby—so the theory went—overcoming the barrier of social class that separated the Church from the working men whom it desired to evangelize), threatened disciplinary measures

---

[4] "Life of Albino Luciani".

[5] From Leo Knowles, *Modern Heroes of the Church* (Huntington, Ind.: Our Sunday Visitor, 2003), and Junno Arocho Esteves, "Pope Francis Officially Declares John Paul I 'Venerable'", *Catholic Herald*, November 9, 2017, https://catholicherald.co.uk/news/2017/11/09/pope-francis-offically-declares-john-paul-i-venerable.

for priests who supported the Communist Party, and suspended some priests who endorsed the liberalization of divorce.

He also supported Pope Paul's encyclical *Humanae Vitae* condemning artificial birth control while taking a patient line with people who had difficulty living up to it. In 1978, when news of the birth of the first "test tube baby", Louise Brown, electrified the world, he extended good wishes to the infant while at the same time upholding the moral norm against artificial insemination. "I do not find any valid reasons to deviate from this norm, by declaring licit the separation of the transmission of life from the marriage act," he said.[6]

On women, Cardinal Luciani insisted that "they are always admirable figures in the Gospels, more so than the apostles themselves." But he added: "Through the will of Christ, women—in my judgment—carry out a different, complementary, and precious service in the church, but they are not 'possible priests'.... That does not do wrong to women."[7]

He also wrote a series of popular essays in which he related faith to life. The essays were cast in the form of letters to famous people, both fictional and real, among them Pinocchio, Figaro, Saint Teresa of Avila, Charles Dickens, Mark Twain, the German poet Goethe, King David, and Jesus. Originally published in a monthly magazine, the pieces were collected in 1976 in a book called

---

[6] *Prospettive nel Mondo*, August 1, 1978; Albino Luciani/Giovanni Paolo I, *Opera Omnia* (Padua: Edizioni Messagero, 1989), 8:571–72.

[7] Quoted by John L. Allen Jr., in "Debunking Four Myths about John Paul I, the 'Smiling Pope'", *National Catholic Reporter*, November 2, 2012, https://www.ncronline.org/blogs/all-things-catholic/debunking-four-myths -about-john-paul-i-smiling-pope.

Illustrissimi, which appeared in an English translation after its author's election as pope.[8]

On becoming pope, John Paul I laid out a six-point program for his pontificate: renew the Church by implementing the Second Vatican Council; complete the revision of the Code of Canon Law; remind Catholics of their duty to preach the Gospel; promote religious unity without compromising doctrine; foster dialogue; seek world peace and social justice. It was a good plan, but he did not live to see it carried out.

It was clear from the start that the new pope wished to do away with pomp and circumstance surrounding the papacy. Among other things, he was the first pope to refer to himself as "I" rather than "we"—a simple step that, along with his agreeable personality and famous smile, contributed to humanizing the papacy. Yet in a September 23 ceremony at the Archbasilica of St. John Lateran, the cathedral of the bishop of Rome, the new holder of that office modestly confessed that he had "not yet 'learned the job' well".[9] And in an Angelus address to the crowd in St. Peter's Square on the Sunday just four days before his death (September 24), he spoke these touching words: "People sometimes say: 'we are in a society that is all rotten, all dishonest.' That is not true. There are still so many good people, so many honest people. Rather, what can be done to improve society? I would say: let each of us try to be good and to infect others with a goodness imbued with the meekness and love taught by Christ."

[8] Albino Luciani, *Illustrissimi: Letters from Pope John Paul I*, trans. William Weaver (Boston: Little, Brown, 1978).

[9] Homily of His Holiness John Paul I: Mass on the Occasion of Taking Possession of the Chair of the Bishop of Rome (September 23, 1978).

On September 28 John Paul I experienced severe pain several times during the day, but he refused to see a doctor. Around 5:30 the following morning, one of the papal apartment's nun housekeepers found him dead—in bed, nightstand light still on, with reading material—perhaps the spiritual classic *The Imitation of Christ*, perhaps the text of a talk he had been scheduled to give that day—still in his hand. Death, it appears, was the result of a pulmonary embolism.[10]

Apparently worried that it would not be edifying to say the dead pope had been found by a woman—the nun housekeeper—who entered his bedroom, the people around him muffed the announcement by giving contradictory accounts of what happened. Soon wild rumors were flying: Pope John Paul had been murdered by the KGB, the CIA, the Mafia, and the Freemasons, as well as officials of the Roman Curia afraid of losing their jobs.

In 1984 a British journalist named David Yallop published a book called *In God's Name*,[11] stringing together what J.N.D. Kelly calls a "tissue of improbabilities"[12] to support the conclusion that curialists and Masons were the perpetrators of the dastardly deed. Five years later, another British journalist, John Cornwell, published *A Thief in the Night*, a volume that systematically exploded Yallop's speculations but concluded that John Paul did indeed suffer from isolation and neglect during his brief time in the Vatican.[13]

---

[10] Sandra Miesel, "A Quiet Death in Rome: Was Pope John Paul I Murdered?", *Crisis Magazine*, April 1, 2009, https://www.crisismagazine.com/2009/a-quiet-death-in-rome-was-pope-john-paul-i-murdered.

[11] David Yallop, *In God's Name* (London: J. Cape, 1984).

[12] Kelly, *Oxford Dictionary of Popes*, 326.

[13] See John Cornwell, *A Thief in the Night: Life and Death in the Vatican* (New York: Penguin Books, 2001); first publication, John Cornwell, *A Thief in the Night: The Mysterious Death of Pope John Paul I* (New York: Viking, 1989).

The process that one day could lead to the Church's formal recognition of Pope John Paul I as a saint began in 1990. Pending its result, Kelly sums up the consensus concerning the smiling pope thus: "The first pope of demonstrably working-class origins, a man of practical common sense who captivated people with his friendly smile, it is impossible to guess what kind of policies he would have pursued had he lived."[14]

LEARNING THE JOB

Pope John Paul I's brief pontificate did not last long enough to produce any significant teaching documents. The excerpt that follows is included here simply because it captures the spirit of this good man so well; it is the conclusion of the homily he delivered at the Mass on the Occasion of Taking Possession of the Chair of the Bishop of Rome in the Archbasilica of St. John Lateran, Rome's cathedral church. As mentioned previously, it was delivered on September 23, 1978—five days before his death.

> And now I have come to the last episcopal duty: "to teach and to observe"; it is the diaconia, the service of guiding and governing. Although already for twenty years I have been Bishop at Vittorio Veneto and at Venice, I admit that I have not yet "learned the job" well.... It is God's law that one cannot do good to anyone if one does not first of all wish him well. On account of this, St. Pius V, on becoming Patriarch of Venice, exclaimed in San Marco: "What would become of me, Venetians, if I did not love you?" I say something similar: I can assure you that I love you, that I desire only to enter into your service

---

[14] Kelly, *Oxford Dictionary*, 326.

and to place the poor powers that I have, however little they are, at the disposal of all.

At this point I must beg the reader's indulgence as I interrupt the narration of high matters for a personal note. I do not know what significance the incident I am about to relate might have (supposing it has any). It may very well have been simply something served up naturally by my subconscious mind in response to recent events in which I had had a very small part. Certainly I have no psychic powers, premonitions and the foretelling of future events are alien to me, and I do not possess even a nodding acquaintance with the paranormal. All I can say is, this really happened.

When Pope Paul VI died, the cardinals of the United States headed to Rome for the conclave that would choose a successor. So did I, having been assigned to serve as their press secretary. The two weeks between my arrival in Rome and the start of the conclave were a period of high excitement and no little tension. The awareness that history was being made filled the busy days and lent a special edge to the scorching heat of that late August in the Eternal City.

As press secretary for the Americans, I found myself a great deal busier than I had expected, arranging briefings for the American press corps, setting up interviews with my cardinals, answering queries. When it was all over, I joined those who had taken part in the voting that elected Pope John Paul in congratulating myself on a job well done and flew home fatigued but satisfied.

Back in Washington, I spent several days catching up on work in the office, sat in on the scheduled meeting of the administrative committee and board of the National Conference of Catholic Bishops (NCCB) and the United

States Catholic Conference (USCC),[15] and then, thinking I owed myself a rest, drove down to the Delaware shore to spend quiet time alone at our family cottage near the ocean. After a day or two of doing nothing except reading a little and loafing, I went to bed one evening pleasantly tired but relaxed, with thoughts of cardinals and conclaves far from my mind.

That night I had two dreams.

In the first dream, I was back in the *Sala Stampa*—the Vatican press office just off St. Peter's Square on the Via della Conciliazione—chatting with an American journalist whom I'll call Walter. He was a European correspondent for a chain of American newspapers, assigned to cover the papal election, and during the run-up to the conclave he and I had become casually friendly. We had often exchanged chitchat and rumors in the *Sala Stampa*, and now here we were in my dream, back in the same place and doing the same thing.

The second dream followed immediately after the first. Now I was walking down the Via della Conciliazione toward the Tiber. Ten or fifteen yards ahead of me were two figures—to the left, Pope John Paul wearing his distinctive white cassock and white capelet, with a white zucchetto on his head, and to his right, a robed and hooded figure. The pope was far shorter than his anonymous companion, not even reaching his waist. Neither of them spoke. In silence they walked side by side toward the river.

At this point in the dream I was awakened abruptly by pounding on the front door (we made it a point to have

---

[15] In 2001, the NCCB and the USCC were combined to form the USCCB (the United States Conference of Catholic Bishops). See "Brief History of the USCCB", USCCB.org, 2019, http://www.usccb.org/about/index.cfm.

no telephone in the cottage back then). Throwing on my bathrobe, I went to see what was going on. There at the door, in the gray light of very early morning, stood the priest of the local parish.

"Yes, Father?"

"Your wife called from Washington. She asked me to come over and tell you ... the pope has died and you have to go back to Rome."

And so I did.

POPE SAINT JOHN PAUL II

(October 16, 1978–April 2, 2005)

The First Postmodern Pope

There were times when it seemed as if Pope John Paul II could do just about anything—do it well, in fact—if he simply set his mind to it. And if reality didn't always measure up to that image, his truly uncommon giftedness did create a special aura around his pontificate, justifying James Hitchcock's assessment that he was "perhaps the most intellectually formidable man ever to ascend the papal throne".[1]

A telegraphic summary of John Paul might go something like this: charismatic contemplative, prophetic voice of orthodoxy, sophisticated intellectual with a deeply held devotion to the Virgin Mary, poet and athlete, foe of Communism and of the consumerist "super development" of the West, philosopher and activist with an actor's flair. And finally, in his painful last years of illness and decline, a figure in whom many beheld a living icon of the suffering Christ.

Coming to the papacy after a long night of confusion and anxiety in the Church capped by the sudden and unexpected death of his predecessor, John Paul II set out

---

[1] James Hitchcock, *History of the Catholic Church* (San Francisco: Ignatius Press, 2012), 509.

to make things right. "Do not be afraid," he reassured the crowd in St. Peter's Square immediately after his election.[2] As Vicar of Christ and Servant of the Servants of God, he took that advice for himself and for nearly twenty-seven years pursued policies that reflected uncommon faith and self-assurance.

Of course, along with countless admirers, he had his critics. Some complained about his teaching on sexual morality, others about his insistence that the Church can't ordain women, or his continued emphasis on celibacy for priests of the Western Church, or his centralized leadership. Sometimes he was blamed for intervening too much in local bishops' affairs, other times—as in the sex abuse scandal—for not intervening enough.[3]

In the end, however, criticism could take nothing away from either the remarkable force of his personality or his extraordinary achievements. George Weigel in his splendid biography situates the source of "conflicting" views of John Paul and his pontificate in the undeniable fact that he was a "sign of contradiction" in relation to certain of the less attractive aspects of postmodernism.

In an intellectual environment in which the human capacity to know anything with certainty is denied, he has taught that universal truths exist, that we can know them, and that in knowing them certain moral duties are

[2] Homily of His Holiness John Paul II for the Inauguration of His Pontificate (October 22, 1978).

[3] Here the critics have a point. Age and illness may provide an excuse, but for whatever reason or combination of reasons, Saint John Paul did not respond as vigorously to the sex abuse scandal as might have been hoped. Apparently he believed that during Pope Paul VI's years it had become too easy for priests quitting the priesthood to obtain laicizations, and to have reacted by making it more difficult, thus also making it harder for bishops to expel abusers from clerical ranks.

laid upon us. At a time when the "personality" is deemed infinitely plastic and in which "human nature" (if its reality is admitted at all) is viewed as a cultural construct, he has defended the idea of a universal human nature and insisted on the *givenness* of the human condition.[4]

But Weigel is quick to reject the idea that John Paul was "a pope *against* modernity and its aspiration to freedom, a pope of 'rollback' and 'restoration'", and his biography makes clear the wrongheadedness of such interpretations.[5]

Karol Jozef Wojtyla was born in Wadowice, an industrial town near Krakow, on May 18, 1920, the second son of Karol Wojtyla, a Polish army officer, and Emilia Kaczorowska Wojtyla. His mother died in 1929, his older brother, Edmund, a physician, in 1932, and his father in 1941. Before World War II he studied philosophy at the Jagiellonian University. When the Nazi occupiers of Poland, seeking to stamp out Polish intellectual life, closed down the university, he worked in a quarry and a chemical plant while acting with an underground theater.

In October 1942, he enrolled in the clandestine seminary conducted by Cardinal Adam Sapieha of Krakow. Following ordination on November 1, 1946, he went to Rome to study at the Angelicum—the Dominican Pontifical University of St. Thomas Aquinas. Returning to Krakow, he did pastoral work, served as a student chaplain, and continued his studies, receiving doctorates from the Jagiellonian in philosophy and theology, after which he joined the philosophy faculty of the Catholic University of Lublin. He also carried on an active apostolate among young lay intellectuals and professional people.

[4] George Weigel, *Witness to Hope* (New York: HarperCollins Perennial, 2005), 6.
[5] Ibid., 7.

On July 4, 1958, while on a kayaking trip with young friends, he received word that Pope Pius XII had named him auxiliary bishop of Krakow. In 1960 he published *Love and Responsibility*,[6] a book presenting Catholic teaching on sexuality and marriage that is said to have influenced Pope Paul VI in writing his encyclical *Humanae Vitae*. (Human sexuality was a subject to which he would return years later as pope in a series of talks developing a distinctive new "theology of the body".) He attended all four sessions of Vatican Council II, speaking several times and helping to write the council's Pastoral Constitution on the Church in the Modern World, Declaration on Religious Freedom, and Decree on the Means of Social Communication.

On December 30, 1963, Pope Paul VI appointed him archbishop of Krakow. In the years that followed, he regularly took part in world Synods of Bishops, held an archdiocesan synod in Krakow, traveled widely in Europe and North America, including the United States, and even visited Australia (for a eucharistic congress), the Philippines, and New Guinea. The pope named him a cardinal on June 26, 1967. His book *The Acting Person*, a densely written philosophical work, was published in 1969.[7] In Lent of 1976 he preached the annual retreat attended by Pope Paul and the Roman Curia. His retreat meditations were published as a volume called *Sign of Contradiction*.[8]

On October 16, 1978, at the conclave following the unexpected death of Pope John Paul I, he was elected 263rd pope, becoming the first non-Italian to hold the

---

[6] Karol Wojtyla, *Love and Responsibility*, English ed. (New York: Farrar, Straus, and Giroux, 1981).

[7] Karol Wojtyla, *The Acting Person*, trans. Andrzej Potocki, English ed. (Dordrecht, Holland/Boston: D. Reidel, 1979).

[8] Karol Wojtyla, *Sign of Contradiction*, English ed. (New York: Seabury Press, 1979).

office since 1522, the first Pole ever, and the youngest pope since Pius IX.

The long pontificate that followed had many high points.

In the front rank of these was his role in the collapse of Soviet Communism and the dissolution of the Soviet empire in Eastern Europe—events in which his name is frequently linked with those of President Ronald Reagan and British Prime Minister Margaret Thatcher. His homecoming to Poland in June 1979—his first visit since his election as pope—sparked a huge upsurge of Polish patriotic and religious sentiment, with thirteen million people turning out to see him, hear him, and pray with him. Reflecting on this historic trip by the Polish pope as it appeared from President Reagan's perspective, historians Lee Edwards and Elizabeth Edwards Spalding write:

> He [Reagan] identified as central weaknesses of the Soviet bloc the denial of religious freedom and the inability to provide consumer goods. He stressed that Pope John Paul II's trip to Poland in 1979 revealed that communist atheism—ruthlessly imposed for decades—had failed to stop the people from believing in God. Reagan noted the pope's language—"Do not be afraid!"—and the size of the crowds at the masses that he celebrated in Krakow, Warsaw, and other Polish cities. In Krakow, the pope's home city, between two and three million people welcomed him, the largest public gathering in the nation's history.[9]

Years later John Paul himself attributed the fall of Soviet Communism largely to the reaction against "the spiritual void brought about by atheism".[10]

---

[9] Lee Edwards and Elizabeth Edwards Spalding, *A Brief History of the Cold War* (Washington, D.C.: Regnery Publishing, 2016), 143.

[10] John Paul II, encyclical letter *Centesimus Annus* (May 1, 1991), no. 24.

Poland was hardly the only place visited by this most-traveled of popes, whose personal program of global evangelization covered a million miles in 104 trips outside Italy. Five times he came to the United States—twice, to address the United Nations—crisscrossing the country from coast to coast. Fidelity to the moral principles embodied in the nation's founding documents was the heart of his message to Americans. For, as he insisted in Baltimore in 1995, "democracy cannot be sustained without *a shared commitment to certain moral truths about the human person and human community.*"[11]

John Paul was an ecumenical and interreligious innovator who, in Eamon Duffy's words, "did more than any single individual in the whole history of Christianity to reconcile Jews and Christians and to remove the ancient stain of anti-Semitism from the Christian imagination".[12] Catholic-Orthodox reunion also was a special cause for him. His May 25, 1995, encyclical *Ut Unum Sint* took the unusual step of inviting other Christian leaders and their theologians to join him in "a patient and fraternal dialogue" on the primacy of the pope and the papal role in fostering and sustaining the unity of the Church.[13]

His many writings as pope reflect his personalist philosophy and his roots in the recent ecumenical council. His was a pontificate filled, says Robert Royal, "less with a new theological system than with a desire to affirm a reading of Vatican II that was both orthodox in terms of continuity with the two-thousand-year-old tradition and confident in facing new challenges from the kind of

---

[11] Apostolic Journey to the United States of America, Homily at Eucharistic Celebration (Oriole Park at Camden Yards, Baltimore, October 8, 1995); emphasis in original.

[12] Eamon Duffy, *Saints and Sinners: A History of the Popes* (New Haven, Conn.: Yale University Press, 2006), 383.

[13] *Ut Unum Sint*, no. 96.

biblical, patristic, and pastoral perspectives most notable in the conciliar documents".[14] Along with important documents on the laity, the dignity of women, and other topics, four of his encyclicals are considered particularly noteworthy: the social encyclical *Centesimus Annus* (May 1, 1991); *Veritatis Splendor* (August 6, 1993), on fundamental moral principles; *Evangelium Vitae* (March 25, 1995), on the life issues; and *Fides et Ratio* (September 14, 1998), on the link between faith and reason.

Veritatis Splendor is the first papal document to give a comprehensive account of the principles underlying the Church's moral teaching on particular issues. Among its features is an extended refutation of the cluster of utilitarian ethical theories known as consequentialism and proportionalism that in the last several decades have been taken up by some Catholic moralists who dissent from the teaching of the Church. Of particular importance in that context is what John Paul says about exceptionless moral norms—norms that identify forms of behavior, such as killing the innocent and adultery, which can never rightly be performed:

> In the question of the morality of human acts, and in particular the question of whether there exist intrinsically evil acts, we find ourselves faced with *the question of man himself*, of his *truth* and of the moral consequences flowing from that truth. By acknowledging and teaching the existence of intrinsic evil in given human acts, the Church remains faithful to the integral truth about man; she thus respects and promotes man in his dignity and vocation. Consequently, she must reject the theories ... which contradict this truth.[15]

---

[14] Robert Royal, *A Deeper Vision: The Catholic Intellectual Tradition in the Twentieth Century* (San Francisco: Ignatius Press, 2015), 240.

[15] *Veritatis Splendor*, no. 83 (emphasis in original).

Pursuing this personalist perspective, the encyclical argues that in upholding the principle of exceptionless moral norms the Church defends and promotes the good of individuals and the well-being of society.

In *Fides et Ratio* (see excerpt at the end of this chapter), John Paul similarly insists that philosophy and faith together are needed as an antidote to postmodern relativism and skepticism. Commenting on this and other papal utterances upholding the proposition that truth exists and can be known, Robert Royal remarks that "if Voltaire were to come back today, he would be shocked to find the greatest defenders of a robust reason sitting on the papal throne."[16]

John Paul also collaborated with Joseph Cardinal Ratzinger, at that time prefect of the Congregation for the Doctrine of the Faith, on two important documents published by the congregation on liberation theology, a school of thought then popular among some Latin American theologians and clergy as well as progressive Catholics in North America and Western Europe. The first document, published in 1984, presented the case against aspects of liberation theology including its advocacy of class conflict and violent revolution as instruments of social progress; while the second, appearing in 1986, gave a positive interpretation of liberationist thinking that stressed "freedom and liberation". Royal says the two documents' grounding in a Christian anthropology that emphasizes human dignity, solidarity, subsidiarity, and the common good gives them "a fruitfulness and a staying power" not found in liberation theology itself.[17]

As noted, in a series of Wednesday audience talks early in his pontificate, John Paul set out a highly original

[16] Royal, *Deeper Vision*, 258.
[17] Ibid, 241.

theological interpretation of human sexuality that has come to be known as the Theology of the Body. Its key ideas are ones that John Paul had been working on for years—even, according to Weigel, during the August 1978 conclave at which Pope John Paul I was elected.[18] The Theology of the Body has provided inspiration for a corps of interpreters and popularizers eager to carry its message to others. Says Weigel: "Few moral theologians have taken our embodiedness as male and female as seriously as John Paul II.... By demonstrating that the dignity of the human person can be 'read' from that embodiedness, he helped enrich the modern understanding of freedom, of sexual love, and of the relationship between them."[19]

John Paul canonized 482 saints—more than all his predecessors combined—and beatified 1,338 others. Among the saints are Father Maximilian Kolbe, Edith Stein, Sister Mary Faustina Kowalska, Mother Katherine Drexel, Padre Pio of Pietrelcina, and Josemaria Escriva, founder of Opus Dei. He also promulgated the revised Code of Canon Law, a project begun in the pontificate of Pope John XXIII.

Of particular note, he commissioned and approved the new *Catechism of the Catholic Church*, the Church's first general catechism in four hundred years. This important project was opposed at the start by some Catholic progressives worried that a comprehensive, definitive new statement of the Church's faith would be an obstacle to the process of never-ending doctrinal change that they favored (a result that was undoubtedly part of what John Paul had in mind). The work nevertheless went ahead over a period of six years, carried on by a commission of cardinals and bishops chaired by Cardinal Ratzinger, who was to succeed Pope

---

[18] Weigel, *Witness to Hope*, 336.
[19] Ibid., 342–43.

John Paul as Pope Benedict XVI, and involving intensive consultation with the world's bishops. The completed *Catechism* now stands as testimony to the vision of John Paul II and his determination to give the Church "a valid and legitimate instrument for ecclesial communion and a sure norm for teaching the faith".[20]

One reason the cardinals had chosen Karol Wojtyla as pope clearly was that, coming after the brief pontificate and sudden death of John Paul I, he radiated physical vigor and good health. But on May 13, 1981, as he was passing through the crowd in St. Peter's Square and greeting people, John Paul II was shot by a Turkish gunman named Mehmet Ali Agca, who apparently acted at the direction of Bulgarian intelligence in a plot orchestrated by Soviet intelligence that feared him—correctly, as events were to show—as a threat to Soviet hegemony in Eastern Europe. The pope's recovery was long and difficult, although eventually he was able to resume his daunting schedule. Starting in the early 1990s, however, he suffered visibly from Parkinsonism, becoming a heroic figure even—or perhaps especially—in his weakness.

At this point I again ask readers to pardon a personal intrusion—this time, in telling the story of Pope John Paul's last days.

Late one Sunday morning in February 2005, I found myself part of a sparse crowd of a few thousand people in St. Peter's Square, trying to keep warm as the damp cold seeped from the old cobblestones into my bones and wondering if it was really worth waiting for Pope John Paul's noontime Angelus—or, more precisely, waiting to see if

---

[20]John Paul II, apostolic constitution *Fidei Depositum* (October 11, 1992), IV. This papal document is published in editions of the *Catechism of the Catholic Church* as an introduction.

there would be a noontime Angelus. For back in January, the pope had been taken to Rome's Gemelli Hospital with what was described as bronchitis, and he had returned to the Vatican just a few days earlier. On a cold, raw, rainy February day like this, no reasonable person could blame him if he skipped the Angelus.

A minute or two before noon, nonetheless the pope's window was opened and the banner bearing the papal coat of arms was lowered beneath it. In a few moments, with the great bells of St. Peter's tolling the noon hour, the Holy Father suddenly appeared at the window, a small figure in white who stood there looking down on us below him. After a pause he began to speak.

The voice was deep, sepulchral. "Like a voice from the tomb" flashed through my mind. Not only that, he was struggling for breath, pausing over every word, every syllable, desperately sucking in air before pressing ahead. And again I found myself thinking: "I wonder if it's a good idea for him to stand there at that open window, doing what he's doing in rotten weather like this."

As a matter of fact, from a merely reasonable point of view, it was a very bad idea. A couple of days later, John Paul was rushed back to Gemelli Hospital. This time a tracheotomy was performed so that he could breathe. Although he returned to the Vatican in a few days, everyone knew the end was approaching. And I, recalling what I had seen and heard that Sunday at noon in St. Peter's Square, knew I had witnessed something more than just a bit of Polish stubbornness on the part of a willful old man: I had been present at an act of heroism: for what John Paul did that morning—standing there in bone-chilling damp cold and struggling to speak—was a duty of office, itself a constituent part of his vocation, and he, like his Lord and Master before him, was determined to live out that vocation to the very end even if it cost him his life.

As it did, at 9:37 P.M. on Saturday, April 2. When the pope's death was announced, the crowd in the square cried, "Santo subito!"—"[Make him a] saint now!" It took nine years—an unusually short time, in fact—but on April 27, 2014, Pope Francis declared him Saint Pope John Paul II.

THE COMPLEX CHALLENGE OF POSTMODERNITY

Finding a few representative paragraphs to excerpt from Pope John Paul's enormous body of work is no easy task, since the materials are not only plentiful but exceptionally rich. The passages that follow, from *Fides et Ratio*, the thirteenth of John Paul's fourteen encyclicals, published in 1998, situate the root of many of the problems of our day in the separation of faith and reason, theology and philosophy, and argue the need for them to come together again and interact for the sake of each. The excerpt also reflects two principal themes of this book: that the world is now experiencing an epochal crisis—a historic turning point—in which modernity painfully gives way to a new era for which we have so far found no better name than "postmodern"; and that we have only begun to experience the consequences of this changeover for our understanding of the human person—which is to say: our self-understanding. Pope John Paul writes:

> The positions we have examined lead in turn to a more general conception which appears today as the common framework of many philosophies which have rejected

the meaningfulness of being. I am referring to the nihilist interpretation, which is at once the denial of all foundations and the negation of all objective truth. Quite apart from the fact that it conflicts with the demands and the content of the word of God, nihilism is a denial of the humanity and of the very identity of the human being. It should never be forgotten that the neglect of being inevitably leads to losing touch with objective truth and therefore with the very ground of human dignity. This in turn makes it possible to erase from the countenance of man and woman the marks of their likeness to God, and thus to lead them little by little either to a destructive will to power or to a solitude without hope. Once the truth is denied to human beings, it is pure illusion to try to set them free. Truth and freedom either go together hand in hand or together they perish in misery....

Our age has been termed by some thinkers the age of "postmodernity". Often used in very different contexts, the term designates the emergence of a complex of new factors which, widespread and powerful as they are, have shown themselves able to produce important and lasting changes.... One thing however is certain: the currents of thought which claim to be postmodern merit appropriate attention. According to some of them, the time of certainties is irrevocably past, and the human being must now learn to live in a horizon of total absence of meaning, where everything is provisional and ephemeral. In their destructive critique of every certitude, several authors have failed to make crucial distinctions and have called into question the certitudes of faith.

This nihilism has been justified in a sense by the terrible experience of evil which has marked our age. Such dramatic experience has ensured the collapse of rationalist optimism, which viewed history as the triumphant progress of reason, the source of all happiness and freedom; and now, at the end of this century, one of our greatest threats is the temptation to despair.

Even so, it remains true that a certain positivist cast of mind continues to nurture the illusion that, thanks to scientific and technical progress, man and woman may live as a demiurge, single-handedly and completely taking charge of their destiny....

To believe it possible to know a universally valid truth is in no way to encourage intolerance; on the contrary, it is the essential condition for sincere and authentic dialogue between persons. On this basis alone is it possible to overcome divisions and to journey together towards full truth, walking those paths known only to the Spirit of the Risen Lord.[21]

---

[21] *Fides et Ratio*, nos. 90–92.

AFTERWORD

British historian Thomas Babington Macaulay was no friend of Catholicism, but in an essay-review in 1840 occasioned by the appearance of Leopold von Ranke's monumental *History of the Popes*, he delivered a remarkable tribute to the Catholic Church. While calling it "a work of human policy"—which Catholics would say is true but only part of the truth—Macaulay went on to write as follows:

The history of that Church joins together the two great ages of human civilization [going on three ages, we would now say, a century and a half later]. No other institution is left standing which carries the mind back to the times when the smoke of sacrifice rose from the Pantheon, and when camelopards and tigers bounded in the Flavian amphitheatre. The proudest royal houses are but of yesterday, when compared with the line of the Supreme Pontiffs. That line we trace back in an unbroken series, from the Pope who crowned Napoleon in the nineteenth century to the Pope who crowned Pepin in the eighth; and far beyond the time of Pepin the august dynasty extends, till it is lost in the twilight of fable. The republic of Venice came next in antiquity. But the republic of Venice was modern when compared with the Papacy; and the republic of Venice is gone, and the Papacy remains.... [The Catholic Church] saw the commencement of all the governments and of all the ecclesiastical establishments that now exist in the

world; and we feel no assurance that she is not destined to
see the end of them all.[1]

There is no reason to jettison this judgment as the Church
and the world traverse the twenty-first century, the third
millennium, and arguably a new, postmodern era in human
history. But there is reason to add to it a bit.

The Catholic Church and the papacy may indeed be
history's two great survivors, but they are also something more. Both enter the third millennium with a mission to the future amounting to a vocation. Here I turn
to *Redemptor Hominis* (The Redeemer of Man), the first
encyclical of Pope Saint John Paul II, dated March 4,
1979, less than five months after his election as pope. The
encyclical set out a vision and an accompanying program
for the extraordinary pontificate that would follow during
the next quarter-century. And already the personalism that
was to be such a notable feature of this pontificate is plain
to see in a passage such as the following, which appears in
the encyclical under the heading "The Human Dimension
of the Mystery of the Redemption":

> Man cannot live without love. He remains a being that
> is incomprehensible for himself, his life is senseless,
> if love is not revealed to him, if he does not encounter
> love, if he does not experience it and make it his own, if
> he does not participate intimately in it. This, as has already
> been said, is why Christ the Redeemer "fully reveals man
> to himself". If we may use the expression, this is the
> human dimension of the mystery of the Redemption. In
> this dimension man finds again the greatness, dignity and
> value that belong to his humanity. In the mystery of the

---

[1] Thomas Babington Macaulay, "Von Ranke", in *Critical and Historical Essays*
(London: J. M. Dent & Sons—Everyman's Library, 1951), 2:38–39.

Redemption man becomes newly "expressed" and, in a way, is newly created. He is newly created! "There is neither Jew nor Greek, there is neither slave nor free, there is neither male nor female; for you are all one in Christ Jesus" (Galatians 3:28). The man who wishes to understand himself thoroughly—and not just in accordance with immediate, partial, often superficial, and even illusory standards and measures of his being—must with his unrest, uncertainty and even his weakness and sinfulness, with his life and death, draw near to Christ. He must, so to speak, enter into him with all his own self, he must "appropriate" and assimilate the whole of the reality of the Incarnation and Redemption in order to find himself. If this profound process takes place within him, he then bears fruit not only of adoration of God but also of deep wonder at himself. How precious must man be in the eyes of the Creator, if he "gained so great a Redeemer" (*Exsultet* at the Easter Vigil), and if God "gave his only Son" in order that man "should not perish but have eternal life" (cf. John 3:16).[2]

It seems appropriate, however, to close where I began, with Romano Guardini. In his great work *The Lord*, Guardini wrote this:

How great the transformation of our conception of man through Christianity, is something we are again beginning to appreciate, now that its validity is no longer generally accepted. Perhaps the moment is not distant in which the Christian ideal, like that of antiquity during the Renaissance, will overwhelm the modern consciousness with its unspeakable plenitude.[3]

---

[2] *Redemptor Hominis*, no. 10.
[3] Romano Guardini, *The Lord* (South Bend, Ind.: Gateway Editions, 1954), 324.

Guardini wrote that many years ago, and his optimism has hardly been borne out by all that has happened since then. But is it not precisely the lesson taught by the eight popes of the twentieth century that this optimism must continue to move Christians in confronting the terrible challenges that lie ahead in postmodern times? And is not the name for this optimism hope?